"[P]erhaps the most famous feminist author
of the interwar period apart from Virginia Woolf."
Choice

VERA BRITTAIN

Vera Mary Brittain was born in Newcastle, England, in 1893. She was educated at Somerville College, Oxford, from which she received both a B.A. and an M.A.

During the First World War she served as a nurse with the Voluntary Aid Detachment in London, Malta, and at the front in France. Her first book, *Verses of a V.A.D.* (1918), grew out of her wartime experiences.

She married the political scientist and philospher George Catlin in 1925; the couple had three children.

The Dark Tide, her first novel, was published in 1923. A decade later came her most famous work, *Testament of Youth: An Autobiographical Study of the Years 1900-1925*. The *Times Literary Supplement* described *Testament of Youth* as "one of the rare books which are a landmark for a whole generation. To young people, and more especially young women, [. . .] Miss Brittain's autobiography interpreted the puzzle of childhood recollections, things incomprehended at the time but of later years never to be forgotten."

In addition to *England's Hour*, which was originally published in 1941, Brittain's many other books include: *Testament of Friendship: The Story of Winifred Holtby* (1940); *Testament of Experience* (1957); *Chronicle of Youth: The War Diary, 1913-1917* (1981); *Chronicle of Friendship: Diary of the Thirties, 1932-1939* (1986); and *Testament of a Peace Lover: Letters from Vera Brittain* (1988).

Throughout her life, Vera Brittain devoted herself to the causes of peace and feminism. She died on 29 March 1970.

ENGLAND'S HOUR

by

VERA BRITTAIN

•

"This is your hour,
and the power of darkness."
St. Luke, 22:53.

•

A Common Reader Edition
The Akadine Press
2002

England's Hour

A COMMON READER EDITION published 2002 by The Akadine Press, Inc.,
by arrangement with The Estate of Vera Brittain.

Cover photograph, by John Freeman:
Cannon Street and St. Paul's Cathedral, 28 October 1941.

A COMMON READER'S LONDON LIBRARY,
A COMMON READER EDITION and fountain colophon
are trademarks of The Akadine Press, Inc.

ISBN 1-585790-55-9

10 9 8 7 6 5 4 3 2 1

I vow to thee, my country—all earthly things above—
Entire and whole and perfect, the service of my love,
The love that asks no questions: the love that stands the test,
That lays upon the altar the dearest and the best:
The love that never falters, the love that pays the price,
The love that makes undaunted the final sacrifice.

And there's another country, I've heard of long ago—
Most dear to them that love her, most great to them that know—
We may not count her armies: we may not see her king—
Her fortress is a faithful heart, her pride is suffering—
And soul by soul and silently her shining bounds increase,
And her ways are ways of gentleness and all her paths are peace.

CECIL SPRING-RICE
British Ambassador to the United States, 1912–1918

(Written January 12, 1918, the last night which he spent at the British Embassy in Washington at the end of his service to England, and little more than a month before his death.)

CONTENTS

PROLOGUE

WHEN THE IDEA of this book first came to me in the summer of 1940, my purpose was to make it a wartime variety of Priestley's *English Journey*. At that time the Battle for Britain was only beginning, and the Battle for London still several weeks ahead. With the intention of travelling round the country and collecting impressions, I made confident plans for a series of journeys to distant parts of this island.

But when the Battle for Britain intensified, and the Battle for London assumed characteristics which few of us had pictured before they appeared, the difficulties of travel combined with the time limit necessarily imposed upon a topical book made the projected long journeys impossible. Moreover, with each day that passed it became clear that the world's eyes were concentrated on London; and such travels as I was able to undertake seemed to show that a tour of the more remote areas of the country would result chiefly in impressions of places which, compared with the dramatic events in London and the South, would differ little from similar impressions in peacetime.

Being a Londoner by adoption, I happened to be in a position to describe those dramatic events. Finally I decided that a book recording the experiences shared by the millions of civilians living in or near London would convey at least as vivid an impression of "England's hour" as an indeterminate tour of districts many miles from the principal battlefield. Hence my object has not been to seek out, like a Special Correspondent, aerial contests, naval catastrophes, domestic tragedies and other front-page stories, but to present, from several different angles, this wartime life as it has appeared to the ordinary London civilian day by day.

In writing, in more than one book, of the last Great War, I was in the position, owing to the lapse of time, of an artist who is able to view a vast landscape in distant perspective. Some day, perhaps, this second great war period of my life may be susceptible to treatment in similar fashion; but the present book, written not only during the war but in the midst of it, has had to forgo the advantages of judgment and comparison which a wide perspective confers. Nevertheless, certain outstanding differences between the two wars which history will emphasise have already become apparent.

The First Great War was fought by bringing into mass conflict many millions of men, whose casualties amounted to a total slaughter so enormous that my generation is correctly described as "lost." So far, in this war, no similar period of mutual annihilation by the picked soldiers of both sides has occurred. The battle is less a struggle between men than a conflict between methods of technical production, and a clash of machines directed by a small number of controlling minds. Above all, it is a competition in propaganda carried out by methods unimagined in the First World War, which are able in a moment to bring the most isolated civilian to the very centre of an international crisis.

In a speech made last August to summarise the consequences of the first year of war, Winston Churchill esti-
mated that for every five men killed or wounded throughout Europe between 1914 and 1915, only one man was
killed or wounded between 1939 and 1940. Far swifter
and greater results than those of the last war have been
achieved in fifteen months of fighting at only a fraction of
the cost in human life.

The nature and scenes of these casualties have also been
different. From 1914 onwards the front was a limited area,
and the lives lost were chiefly those of young men between eighteen and forty. To-day, the failure of men and
women to work with sufficient vigour for the lasting peace
that they might have achieved between ten and twenty
years ago, has brought whole nations into the struggle.
The front is everywhere owing to the moral inability,
shared by every great power, to refrain from the manufacture and use of the bombing aeroplane. In addition to
capital cities, all the towns, villages, and hamlets of every
combatant country are potential battlefields. Not only the
workmen in the factories, but the mothers in their homes,
run risks comparable to those of the fighting soldier in the
First Great War. Though a much larger number of innocent and defenceless civilians have died in 1940 than in
1915, from a biological standpoint the casualties are better distributed. Even amongst the many Londoners who
have lost their homes and seen death come to their families, I have never heard the complaint that wars exclu-
sively destructive of young men are preferable to the
shared risks and sorrows of the present. On the other
hand, the far wider experience of distress and upheaval is
causing, amongst hitherto inert millions, some hard thinking about the cost of modern warfare to the common citi-

zens of all countries which will have its effect when the voice of the people is again able to make itself heard.

Finally, the part played in this war by England herself has been wholly different from her share in the last. Except for the slight damage done by the occasional visits of the large slow Zeppelins of which our past fears now seem ludicrous, England's first ordeal was mainly vicarious. Her suffering was the anguish of detached suspense; it was embodied in the long-drawn anxiety of thousands for the husbands, fathers, brothers, and sons who had vanished overseas to some far-off unimaginable existence of which only the few women who went abroad as nurses and canteen workers had the remotest conception. Again and again, the difference between the lives led by soldiers at the front and by civilians at home caused a barrier of inconceivable experience to harden between the fighting men and the women who loved them.

To-day both suffering and suspense are universal in England herself. The painful ache of anxiety is felt as often by husbands for wives as by wives for husbands. There is no emotional barrier between men and women, parents and children, the old and the young, since the battle is shared by all ages and both sexes. Our island is no longer a detached unscarred participant sharing in the conflict only through the adventures of masculine youth; the marks of war, so deeply inscribed upon London, are written on her towns and villages too. Often they appear more clearly in the eyes of her women, and sometimes, alas! of her children, than upon the faces of her men.

Apart from these three conspicuous distinctions between two wars which are emphasized by every detail here recorded, this book draws no conclusions and attempts no final judgments. It endeavours to give the sole impression possible at this stage—that of a "close-up" study of the past fifteen months as experienced by civilians living in a limited area of the small island which has borne, for thirteen momentous weeks, the burden and heat of a huge world conflict.

Only in the last two chapters have I struggled towards a perspective which I cannot believe that the future will substantially change.

V. B.

November 9, 1940

Note: This book had gone to the printers before the severe series of provincial air-raids which started in the latter half of November had begun. I am, of course, aware that long before the war came to London, many towns and cities in the North-East, South-East, and South-West of England had experienced continuous aerial bombardment. I had intended to visit all these areas, but lack of time combined with the personal problem created for me by the bombardment of London, compelled me, to my regret, to abandon this more comprehensive scheme.

ENGLAND'S HOUR

1. DISPLACEMENT OF POPULATION

THE SUMMER OF 1939 has been one of the wettest in English memory.

Throughout July and the first three weeks of August, the rains have descended and the floods have come, turning the New Forest into a swamp and its gentle springs to angry rivulets. The troops encamped in the Forest for "training" have all departed for indoor quarters, when suddenly the weather changes. The last week of the uneasy peace which Europe has struggled for twenty years to maintain becomes one of the loveliest on record. A golden light shines benignly upon Hampshire's gorse and heather; the Isle of Wight gleams like a jewel across the blue channel of Southampton Water.

In the garden of our New Forest cottage where we are spending the summer holidays, the children and I count five Peacocks and seven Red Admirals dancing above the Michaelmas daisies. From distant cottage gardens, the faint smell of bonfires which drifts across England in early autumn hangs on the air. The mellow serenity of lanes and woods makes the gathering crisis in Europe seem only the more malevolent and incongruous.

Rumours begin to fly round our hamlet. The soldiers who left their muddy tents and duckboards are now re-

ported to have sailed for an "unknown destination."
Hundreds of Americans are said to be leaving England;
someone has seen the German liner *Europa* passing Southampton at full speed without stopping to disembark her
passengers. The evacuation of children from London and
other threatened cities is rumoured to have begun; a
neighbour has watched a trainload of boys and girls passing through Brockenhurst. In this and other Forest villages, all available rooms at the country hotels are suddenly booked up. At two hours' notice, a young friend
from London descends with her nurse and baby upon our
cottage. Hurrying in the seventh-hand Baby Austin to
Lyndhurst, our nearest "town," we lay in an extra stock
of sheets and crockery. We also buy black sateen and ply-
wood for darkening our windows.

On August 24th, the news of the German-Soviet Pact is
published, and the Crisis in Embryo becomes the Crisis
Proper.

"I can't guess," writes my author friend from Berkshire
who is anxiously wondering whether to accompany the
P.E.N. Conference to Sweden, "what this Russian business means, but I suppose that at the least it quickens the
pace . . . The last few days have been a nightmare, trying
to find homes for refugees who are turned out because
the rooms where they have been receiving hospitality are
needed for evacuated children. Reading has just been put
on the list of places to which children may not be evacuated, so that all the arrangements made for this district
are upside down, and it looks as though we'd have to take
in four instead of the two children we agreed to take. I
don't know where we'll put them, or on what! . . . In all
this sunshine, the wireless announcements are fantastic.
Can you remember 1914 at all clearly? I seem to remember

much more excitement. There doesn't seem any war fever about now, thank God."

Two days later, a warm beautiful Saturday, my son and daughter and I stand on the village green outside our cottage, and watch the Crisis Personified move along the Bournemouth-Southampton-London road two hundred yards from our door. From morning till night the road is alive with a restless ribbon of traffic—lorries filled with troops; long-distance "Relief" buses crammed with passengers; small cars packed with children, their parents, perambulators and cots; motor-cycle dispatch riders; vans from furniture repositories loaded with household goods. Everyone on holiday seems to be going home, and everyone at home to be leaving it for somewhere else. No doubt the scene could be paralleled on any other highroad in England, for every civilian now knows that this time he, as much as any soldier, will become part of the enemy's objective.

After that great exodus, all activities other than those of the Government and the military machine seem universally at a standstill. Normal holiday occupations are suspended while the nation waits on events. The countryside is empty; the lovely Hampshire beaches are deserted. The strange waiting silence seems more sinister than the previous racket of traffic. It continues for days while the B.B.C. announcers impart ever more disastrous information in cultured reassuring voices, and conclude each broadcast with a new list of instructions and exhortations. Letters and newspapers begin to arrive late. Telegrams are delayed for hours; long-distance trunk calls have to be registered in advance; subscribers are urged not to use the telephone except for urgent business.

"What shall we do?" blankly inquire the children, usually so resourceful in self-entertainment. They can no more concentrate on their games than we on the work in hand.

When the newspapers do arrive, we read them carefully, studying the news, the editorials, even the correspondence—which varies, as always, from personal suggestions for political programmes to apt quotations from Plato or Horace. One distinguished correspondent writes to plead for generosity to dachshunds, pointing out that these small elongated dogs have been British-bred for generations. Behind the letter lies the implication (of which the distinguished correspondent appears unconscious) that, had they been German-bred, ill-treating them wouldn't have mattered.

We wander through the Forest to the Roman bridge across the placid stream known as Highland Water. The rivulet tinkles gently over the stones beneath the beech-trees; a celestial light illumines the deepening purple of the heather. We walk back a little wearily, tired of the crises which have destroyed the hope and impaired the beauty of the late lovely summer.

Finally I put Hilary to bed, and decide to take Richard to the Lyndhurst cinema. As we walk there, workmen with paint-pots and huge flat brushes are painting white lines down the centre of the road in preparation for the impending black-out. The little picture theatre is showing Shaw's *Pygmalion* to a crowded house. Before the big film comes a newsreel, which provides—as so often at small country cinemas—news that is not exactly of the "hot topical" variety.

Though the terms of the German-Soviet Pact have been known for five days, the newsreel shows the British Military Mission leaving some weeks earlier to negotiate with Russia. The operator, perceiving the situation, winds this section of the reel up to top speed, but the complacent, smiling faces of the British representatives come out as clearly as the announcer's suave conclusion: "And we wish them every success in their friendly talks with the Soviet Government."

Richard and I wait for the reaction from the village audience. Will it be boos, hisses, catcalls? It comes—a spontaneous and unanimous burst of derisive laughter.

Three days afterwards, the Germans—followed by the Russians—march into Poland. All day long we feel slightly sick, as one does when people die. I offer myself as a blood donor, and learn from the woman officer taking names of volunteers that children from Portsmouth are expected at a near-by village, Emery Down.

"To-morrow," she adds, "they're going to be evacuated from Southampton."

When to-morrow comes, my husband learns that he must take a midday train for an urgent appointment in Lancashire. We drive the Baby Austin to Southampton; an outgoing surge of traffic obliges us to leave it some distance from the station. The booking hall is an pandemonium of tearful parents, mingled with young men joining their regiments. Platform tickets are temporarily suspended; only those actually travelling may pass through the barrier. On the platform stand the children in their school hats and coats; with the imperturbable resignation of youth born into a dangerous world, they wait patiently in line carrying their little satchels.

We learn that no cross-country trains are running, so Martin must go to Rochdale via London. He says goodbye to me at the barrier.

"Well," he remarks grimly, "this is the first time I've seen an English town which reminded me of Madrid in the Civil War."

"You'll see plenty more," I tell him.

2. SEPTEMBER 3, 1939

IT IS SUNDAY MORNING. In the small study of the forest cottage, the children and I sit waiting for the "important announcement" forecast at ten o'clock by the B.B.C.

Outside the window stretches the New Forest, green, sunlit and still. During the tense days before us, its lovely tranquillity will defeat the efforts of my imagination to picture the agony of the population in devastated Poland, the terror of children drowned in the stricken *Athenia*. The quiet warmth of the gorse and heather, the scarlet butterflies flitting above the goldenrod in the cottage garden, make the size and significance of the coming catastrophe impossible to apprehend.

A half-grown forest pony, born during the spring, scampers across the dry turf beneath the giant beeches.

"Sweet foal!" cries my little daughter, more interested, at nine years old, in ponies than in political calamity. Jumping up, she leans over the creeper-covered window-ledge to watch the graceful red-brown creature gallop downhill towards its placid mother who nibbles the long lush grass at the edge of the empty road.

From the distant somnolence of a forest town, the church bells summon Hampshire men and women to worship the Author of Peace and the Lover of Concord. Nine months afterwards, those bells will be silenced on Sunday mornings. They will be dedicated only to the strange task of calling a people expecting invasion to the capture of Germans landing by parachute.

The hour, 11.15, comes near. With a sense of precipitating the advance of doom, I turn the knob of the radio. In a moment the silence of the little room is broken by a familiar voice—an old voice, harsh and arrogant, though now it trembles.

"This morning," announces Neville Chamberlain from the Cabinet Room at 10 Downing Street, "the British Ambassador in Berlin handed the German Government a final note, stating that, unless we heard from them by eleven o'clock that they were prepared at once to withdraw their troops from Poland, a state of war would exist between us.

"I have to tell you now that no such undertaking has been received, and that consequently this country is at war with Germany.

"You can imagine what a bitter blow it is to me that all my long struggle to win peace has failed . . ."

Awed and a little bewildered, Richard and Hilary sit on either side of me listening. Fortunately for themselves, they are spared the memories of an older war generation. They cannot see the pictures haunting my mind—the waiting darkness of a long-ago August midnight suddenly broken by excited voices crying that England's ultimatum to Germany has expired, the November morning tumult of London crowds clamorously welcoming an Armistice won for them by a lost generation of men who died in a war to end war.

"Twenty years," I am thinking. "For twenty years my friends and I, who learned from the suffering and disillusion of those four lifelong years that only the Kingdom of

Heaven within us has power to overcome the brute forces of evil, have also worked for peace and the triumph of human sanity. We worked with more faith, more sincerity, more inspiration, than Neville Chamberlain, yet the world has come back to this. How was it we achieved so little? Where and why did we fail?"

I do not realize how clearly my expression reflects the painful conflict of my thoughts, but Hilary perceives it. Impulsively she flings her warm dimpled arms round my neck, almost licking my face in the puppy-like exuberance of her affection.

"Poor Mummie! Don't cry, Mummie! It'll be all right in the end, really it will!"

For a moment, looking at eleven-year-old Richard, my misgivings increase. Shall we fight until his generation, too, is caught and devoured by the striding Juggernaut which hatred and fear have created? Then, like a drowning man who suddenly perceives land close beside him, I struggle out of the black engulfing waters.

"Hilary's quite right," I tell myself. "This is no time for tears. It is a time for resolution, and the rededication of ourselves to those ideal ends whose fulfilment we shall now never see. Let us, who have striven unavailingly for peace, remember and repent of the wrongs that England has done, and her share in the destructive follies which have again helped to plunge the world in sorrow. But let us remember that she has done great and wise and merciful things as well, and will achieve them again if we, her people, are determined that she shall. There is work for us now, in mitigating the burden laid upon her and her citizens, of whom we are part, and in striving to maintain the nobler values of civilisation through the dark hours before us. Let us keep our heads and lift up our hearts—

not for the negative purpose of destroying the great nation which has allowed itself to be captured by a doctrine of cruelty and vengeance, but in order that we may work the better

> "for some idea, but dimly understood,
> Of an English city never built with hands,
> Which love of England prompted and made good."

3. BLIMPS ON THE COAST

THE DAY AFTER war has broken out, Richard points to six barrage balloons which are visible from our cottage. Fantastic aerial monsters, they have crept one by one from Southampton round the coast. The next day the British bomb the Kiel Canal, and at night, in expectation of reprisals, a brilliant constellation of searchlights competes with the stars above Calshot. Standing outside our cottage in the darkness scented by damp earth and heather, we watch a dozen luminous pencils crossing and recrossing one another over the sea ten miles away.

In a few days' time, local rumours of air-raids percolate through our village. London, Portsmouth, Southampton, are said to have been bombed, "but of course it wasn't on the wireless." Vigorously my young cook-housekeeper expresses her disapproval of these "jitterbugs."

"I'm not going over to B. any more," she tells me. "They spend the whole time there working each other up with horrible tales. I'm not going to believe anything unless I hear it from the B.B.C.!"

When the holidays are nearly over, I take the children to Bournemouth to buy some new school clothes. Like other health resorts at a safe distance from London and similar danger spots, Bournemouth is booming. In the prosperous-looking streets, throngs of visitors run to and fro conspicuously carrying their gas-masks. The containers reflect the personality of the owner; they vary from biscuit-tins and cardboard boxes to elaborate black suède carriers edged with scarlet leather. Along the sunny front on the cliff tops, all the hotels are crowded. The shopkeepers, coining money, privately welcome the war. They do not realise how soon their own hour of catastrophe will come upon them, nor dream that, in less than twelve months, the South Coast will become the front line and its tourist traffic vanish.

A week later I am in Southampton on business at the American Consulate. Unlike the towns, the little Forest railway stations between Bournemouth and Southampton already wear a desolate appearance; they were made for pleasure, and the sudden descent of business in the shape of troops and military stores has overwhelmed their small leisurely staffs. Southampton, too, looks deserted except for its main streets; ubiquitous piles of sandbags already give it the appearance of a city on active service. Many small gunboats and cruisers pack the harbour. In the Cunard-White Star dock lies the *Mauretania,* painted grey and so changed in appearance that from a distance I mistake her for a battleship.

"Pardon me," apologises the United States Vice-Consul after keeping me waiting for half-an-hour, "but I'm still very busy evacuating American citizens."

Agreeably co-operative, he accepts my application for a renewal of my re-entry permit into the United States which will enable me to fulfil a future lecture contract. Having filed the application, I am now confronted with the difficulty of forwarding the necessary fee to Washington in a country from which money may no longer be exported. I have no alternative to sending the entire document to my bank manager in New York, asking him to pay the fee. As I mail it, I wonder what happens to would-be cross-Atlantic travellers who have no banking account in America.

There are still children, I notice, in the back streets of Southampton in spite of the official exodus. The newspapers are filled with evacuation stories from "the heart of Hertfordshire" or "somewhere in Sussex," but already there are signs that the scheme is not wholly successful. Sometimes the householders, rigidly exclusive and too much hidebound by class distinctions to offer friendship to families with a different social background, have been the factor at fault. At other times the billeting officers have shown a singular lack of imagination—as on the occasion when they imposed a family of five mental defectives on a seventy-year-old rural antiquarian, who was obliged in turn to evacuate his china and his valuable first editions.

But government departments which have displayed the usual bureaucratic indifference to the human element are not solely to blame for the hitches in the scheme. The responsibility must be shared by all of us who have permitted such vast differences of standards to exist that certain sections of the community cannot meet and mingle. Among dozens of stories, one especially illustrates the sorrowful truth that one half of England did not know how the other half lived.

A benevolent motherly spinster took in two little sisters of ten and twelve from a dockyard slum. Putting them into her second-best bedroom, she left them to get undressed for the night. Going up later to tuck them in bed and comfort possible homesickness, she found no trace of the children. Thinking that they were playing a trick on her, she looked in vain behind screen, cupboard, and curtains.

"You bad little things!" she finally called out. "Where are you hiding?"

A small voice answered from under the bed. "We're here. Isn't this where we're supposed to be?"

In a household such as that, where children accustomed to sleeping on the floor beneath their parents' bed are treated kindly and taught middle-class standards of conduct, the evacuees will probably stay. What will be the effect on their own homes when the war is over and they return to their families?

The first holidays of wartime are ended, and Richard, Hilary, and I begin to pack. Just before he returns to school, my son receives an unexpected gift from the owner of a small Chelsea bookshop who for two or three years has supplied him with stamps for his cherished collection. Enclosed in a letter to his "Dear Laddie," the old man sends three rare stamps, worth eleven shillings—a small fortune to Richard. Sorrowfully he writes that he may be compelled to close down, as all his best customers have left London for the country. He started his little shop with money made from selling his own stamp collection after the war of 1914, and now another war has ruined it. He is typical of too many "small men" whose wealthy patrons have fled from danger at the first whisper of its wings.

Richard, much distressed by his old friend's misfortune, spends half the morning laboriously composing a letter of sympathy on the typewriter.

"The trouble about your buissness," he writes, "is indeed a drastic stop, but I shall continue to buy from you to the best of my ability."

We take Hilary back to school in Swanage—still a peaceful Dorset coast town where even Air Raid Precautions have hardly penetrated. Nine months hence, as part of the defence area with bombs and aeroplanes falling round it, Swanage will become a battle zone for the first time since the days of Alfred the Great, and many of its fourteen schools will be numbered with war's educational casualties.

The next day, using up our last stores of unrationed petrol, we drive Richard also back to his school in the Malvern hills. The ancient Baby Austin, in protest against being expected to do two hundred miles in a day, breaks down once or twice, but eventually deposits him there. Richard's headmaster, a wise and sensitive man who is a history specialist, listens gravely to my conventional expression of sympathy on the problems of teaching the young in a constantly war-ridden world.

"After all," he comments, "there have been ages when the job was even more difficult. Think what it must have meant for a boy to have grown up during the Thirty Years' War!"

Coming back to the New Forest the car excels itself, but in spite of its efforts twilight descends before we reach Salisbury. For the last twenty miles from Salisbury to Lyndhurst, we drive without lights through the gathering darkness. We cannot see the signposts except by getting out of the car and striking a match; we are guided away from the ditch only by the white lines which divide the road, and spring into startling clearness whenever the car passes through the deep shadows of the woods. By the time we reach home I feel cramped and dizzy, but we arrive, miraculously, without mishap.

Now that the children's holidays are over, London and work demand our presence. We make ready to leave the Forest with its reminders of Richard and Hilary; and I pay a final visit to their "submarine"—the big fallen tree in the wooded glade over the brow of the hill where I can still picture their small ghosts playing. Martin joins me and we walk through the Forest towards Brockenhurst; it is a quiet afternoon, and no breath of wind stirs the interlacing boughs of the woodland beeches. Coming back, we pass a little group of cottages at the corner of the glade; from their kitchens emerges a smell of peat-fires which mingles with the garden scent of ripe red apples and scarlet dahlias. In the lane a little boy is twisting himself blithely on a homemade swing above a woodpile.

How much more tragic, I remark to Martin, the war seems here than in London; the contrast is so poignant between the lovely, stable, civilised things which are the real essence of people's lives, and the carnage and destruction that threatens their very existence. All this week, in the September sunshine, our own garden with its sunflowers and Michaelmas daisies has been a royal glory of gold and purple, jewelled with the flitting beauty of the Forest butterflies. So many friends were meant to see and enjoy these treasures during late summer week-ends, but because of the war only a few have been here. We discuss the threat made by man's ruthless game of power politics to this innocent loveliness, and perceive the essence of war's tragedy in the peace and fragrance of the little garden.

4. WINTER BLACK-OUT

THOUGH LONDON IS HALF DESERTED, we find it more tolerable than the country. In spite of closed offices and West End mansions decorated with "To LET" notices which vainly advertise their attractions to non-existent buyers, it is worth confronting potential danger to know what is happening from hour to hour.

With the corner house next door unoccupied and the three on the other side of us for sale we feel somewhat isolated, but at last we are freed from the wild rumours which speed like invisible banshees round the rural areas.

From the heart of the city right out to such "dormitory" neighbourhoods as Hampstead and Ealing, building contractors are now at work on A.R.P. shelters and sandbagged posts. Everywhere windows are decorated with long strips of paper-strapping to prevent the splintering effect of "blast" from bombs; wooden barricades and piles of sandbags protect the doorways of hotels and flats. In Knightsbridge and other main shopping centres associated for generations with comfort and security, we find arrow-shaped orange notice-boards incredibly inscribed "To the Trenches." After standing on Chelsea Bridge one autumn evening at sunset, we realize that the barrage balloons above Southampton are a mere sample compared with the

shining galaxy defending London. When we "black-out"
our house on Chelsea Embankment, we are impressed by
the increase in the price of the voluminous A.R.P. material
required to conceal its large eighteenth-century windows.

"Surely," I remark to Robert, our houseman, as we both
gaze dubiously at the yards of black sateen, "this is the
same material that I paid sevenpence for at Lyndhurst?"

"It's about the same," he responds impartially, "but it's
one and twopence here."

As November comes in with its long foggy nights,
torches are at a premium, and spare batteries unobtainable even from Boots' or Woolworth's. White paint, also,
is heavily in demand; the local authorities use it to make
lines on tree-trunks, curbs, gateposts, and steps. We purchase a pot of luminous paint and, assiduous as habitual
drunkards, use it to decorate the keyhole and the front
doorbell.

So far, the black-out is the wartime measure which
most conspicuously affects civilians, who find it difficult to
recognise familiar roads, and do not always know their
own houses. In the main streets, beneath winter stars for
the first time clearly visible, they cannonade with strangers,
tumble into piles of sandbags, and sprain their ankles falling over the curb. A few, with practice, gradually develop
a sixth sense which is halfway between the sense of touch
and the sense of smell. One pitch-black November night
I find my way on foot from Oxford Street through Bond
Street to a party at the Mayfair Hotel off Piccadilly, and
cannot imagine how I should have arrived at my destination without the help of this developing instinct.

Every other sense has to be on the alert as well, and
some people, especially amongst the older generation,
never achieve sufficient concentration to walk successfully

through the darkness. The hospitals evacuated for civilian air-raid casualties find work looking after the casualties due to the black-out, which exceed in number the British military casualties of the war. Throughout this period, the baffling quiet of the false lull enshrouds the sea, the air, and the Maginot Line. Some American journalists write scornfully of a "phony war"; neither they nor the Allies realise as yet that the Nazis are using these peaceful months to perfect their military machine, and to entangle those countries destined to be conquered in a network of Fifth Column activities.

On November 11th, the occasion that we have known so long as Armistice Day celebrates its coming of age. In London—officially owing to the danger of air raids—the usual celebrations at the Cenotaph are curtailed. Perhaps, even for the least imaginative bureaucrat, that memorial ceremony would have suggested too acutely mankind's betrayal of its sacrificial youth, who perished to make the world safe for democracy, and instead helped to establish the most ruthless dictatorships which this world has known.

In an office which was once the scene of much hopeful activity, some of my friends from the peace movement are speculating on the future of the Cenotaph.

"If we win this war," asks one, "shall we have another Armistice Day, and a new monument to 'The Glorious Dead'? Or shall we again contrive to end the war at the eleventh hour of the eleventh day of the eleventh month, so as to save inventing another ceremony?"

"Ever seen the French monument to the dead of 1870 in the churchyard at Camiers?" inquires another. "After the last war, they economised by adding a brief inscription commemorating the heroes of 1914 to 1918. We shan't have any money when we've won this war—so we shall probably just have to do the same."

Sometimes I wonder whether the historians of to-morrow, for whom this bitter twentieth century will represent no more than a watch in the night, are likely to regard the first Armistice, though it lasted for two decades, as anything more than a pause in the long struggle between Western and Central Europe. To look upon it in this way will be too drastic a simplification of twenty years of lost opportunity. It will mean forgetting that 1918 left the victorious Allies with the remaking of Europe in their hands; it will overlook the fact that for fifteen years the possibility of saving the world from another disastrous war remained, had enlightened and imaginative statesmanship existed to take advantage of it. For the generation, at any rate, which was born in the closing years of the nineteenth century, those two decades represented a large and important slice of life. They carried us from an adventurous youth to an eventful middle-age; they gave us an interval in which to dream of a peaceful, secure, and prosperous world which we—now doubly the war generation—are never likely to see in our time.

Ten years ago, my generation hopefully believed that the worst consequences of the Great War were over. We looked forward to a period of recovery in which to lay the foundations of that warless society which our lovers and brothers and friends had given their lives to establish. With a sense of confidence such as we had not known since our childhood, we bought our little homes, founded our little businesses, got married, and had children.

To-day, with the coming of another war, too many of those businesses have been closed, those homes abandoned. But our children remain. We gave them birth in our brief hour of hope that human faith and common sense would honour the sacrifice of a dozen nations' dead. Now that this hope has been shattered, the obligation lies heavily upon us to save them from death—not the death of the body alone, but the death of the spirit.

We can do this only by bequeathing to them, as part of our legacy of crowded experience, the vision of a united community which some of us salvaged from the First Great War, and for a while believed we could realise through that tragically untried experiment in international co-operation known as the League of Nations. The League failed, and war has returned, but the vision cannot die. Like Cicero to his friend Atticus, there are men and women still ready to say: "I care more for that long age which I shall not see, than for my own small share of time."

During the dark, interminable evenings, many English families, tired of travelling through the cold blackness to clubs and restaurants, come to know their homes as they have never known them before. Publishers and editors rejoice; these fireside nights will inevitably mean a large increase in reading. The libraries flourish; sixpenny "Penguins" with white covers carrying scarlet titles appear in their hundreds on every bookstall and are eagerly purchased.

I can seldom join the fireside readers, for during the late autumn I have to fulfil an intimidating series of lectures and meetings rashly undertaken some months before the war. In November I travel to Manchester, Birmingham, Nottingham, Liverpool, Reading, Exeter, and Portsmouth, by trains which are slow, crowded, and devoid of restaurants. Before nightfall the blinds are drawn down, and the railway carriage, if lighted at all, is illumined by a blue pinpoint of light not strong enough to enable me to dis-

tinguish the features in the pale ovals which are my neighbours' faces.

At Portsmouth, a number of brick and concrete shelters
are already going up in the streets. They will be needed
later, for Portsmouth—like London, Southampton, Bristol,
and other dockyard towns—will find itself in the centre of
the Blitzkrieg. From Portsmouth I visit Hilary at Swanage
for her half-term holiday; I have gone to Richard in Herefordshire the week before. The return train to London
takes five hours, and provides neither heat, light, nor food.
Sometimes half dozing, sometimes wide-awake, I sit in the
darkness thinking lugubriously of the work that I should
be able to do on that long journey if I could only see. Outside the carriage window, a brilliant full moon makes the
darkened country clearer than dawn; in the ghostly light,
Southampton's cranes and chimneys appear as grotesque
phantoms with arms raised in supplication. Recalling Martin's description of trains in Russia, I wonder how closely
British railways may come to resemble them before war is
over.

Towards the end of the year, my journeys, like the winter, grow colder. A five-day December series in the North
is accompanied, in rapid succession, by snow, frost, fog,
and heavy rain. In Lancashire, sleet-showers hold up the
train; on the Yorkshire hills between Burnley and Harro-
gate, the snow already lies so deep that a snow-plough has
to clear the roads. Outside the small radius reached by
infrequent coal fires, hotels and houses seem cold as the
poles. At Bradford my hostess and I, finding the black-out
increased by heavy mist, look for half an hour in streets
normally familiar to her for the hall where I am booked to
speak. In Hampshire, our New Forest cottage is surrounded
by a swamp which defies the efforts of any car to approach
nearer than twenty yards from the door.

Though my conscience is challenged by posters all over London which inform me, "Children are safer in the country—keep them there," I venture to bring Richard and Hilary to town for Christmas. War, for them, does not spoil the day, and the experiment seems justified until, early in January, rumours of a Nazi invasion of Holland because the water defences are frozen startles Europe for several days. This time, the invasion does not occur, but the family gives way to a sigh of relief when Richard and Hilary are safely back at school.

With the New Year, as though war were not in itself a sufficient ordeal, the coldest winter for more than forty years creeps over England. Magnetic mines, Germany's newest "secret weapon," are blown all over the Channel by the stormy winds. As the harsh days slowly grow longer, my author friend writes me from the country that she is working with numb fingers in a room where, in spite of the fire, there is ice inside the windows.

"It is still bitterly cold here," she reports. "So cold, my brains seem frozen in my head."

All over Britain, the poorly protected pipes freeze and burst, and the population shivers beside its small fires of rationed coal. The 21st of January is the coldest day ever recorded in England. On the 24th, the temperature is 5 below zero in the Malvern hills, and Richard's school is snow-bound. In London, the snow falls and lies deep, hard as iron beneath 25 degrees of frost. The Thames is frozen over at Kingston and for eight miles between Teddington and Sunbury; twelve inches of ice cover lakes and reservoirs; in Hyde Park the population skates on the Serpentine.

In mid-February the snow is still falling as the year which has opened so grimly marches on to its fate.

5. THE BLITZKRIEG ARRIVES

AFTER THEIR OWN PHENOMENAL WINTER, my friends in America are shivering and aching for warmer weather, yet every gleam of sunshine fills them with a miserable, vicarious apprehension. By no desire of its own, this great nation is playing the role of spectator at a bullfight.

"The same spring," grimly comments an editorial in the *Detroit Free Press*, "that unlocks the daisies in America, unlocks the poppies in Flanders Field."

"Never," writes a regular correspondent from Minneapolis, "have I so longed for spring—or dreaded its coming more." Everybody, she tells me, is echoing the inquiry which appeared one March Sunday in the *New York Times* above the picture of an air battle over a North Sea convoy: "Will Spring Signal the Launching of Long-Threatened Aerial Warfare?"

They have not many weeks, now, to await a reply to their question. One evening at the beginning of April, the news of the Scandinavian occupation comes over the radio, and incredibly, almost overnight, Denmark and Norway vanish from the map of Europe's independent states. Norway calls upon Britain for aid, but the Norwegian campaign contributes a series of unavailing tragedies to the history of the war. Early in May, the local superiority of the German Air Force compels the British contingents to evacuate Aandalsnes and Namsos.

A sharp debate follows in the House of Commons to determine whether England has a leadership sufficiently dynamic to enable her to play her part in the dangerous crises which have already begun. Neville Chamberlain, in a long defensive speech, attempts to answer his critics and to minimize Britain's loss of world prestige. He is attacked by Sir Roger Keyes, who declares that the Navy has been "let down" by the cowardice of Whitehall. And by L. S. Amery, who quotes with great effect the words of Oliver Cromwell to the Long Parliament: "You have sat here too long for any good you are doing. Depart, I say, and let us have done with you. In the name of God, go!"

Next day the battle is renewed by Herbert Morrison, who declares that because of the gravity of recent events the Opposition feels compelled to divide the House at the end of the debate. Neville Chamberlain accepts the challenge and appeals to his supporters: "At least we shall see who is with us and who is against us. I call upon my friends to support us in the Lobby to-night!" Rising not only from the Opposition Liberal benches, but from the mists of the past in which he was "Victory Premier," David Lloyd George attacks Chamberlain for seeking to compass a situation so critical within the narrow confines of personal status:

"It is not a question of who are the Prime Minister's friends. It is a far bigger issue. The Prime Minister must remember he has met this formidable foe of ours in peace and in war, and he has always been worsted. He is not in a position to do it on the ground of friendship. He has appealed for sacrifice. The nation is prepared for it so long as it has leadership. I say now, solemnly, that the Prime

Minister can give an example of sacrifice, because there is
nothing that would contribute more to victory in this war
than that he should sacrifice the Seals of Office."

At the end of a long speech by Winston Churchill in defence of the Admiralty's policy in the Norwegian campaign, the House is divided. When the count is made, the
Government majority is only eighty-one; numerous well-
known Conservatives, such as Lady Astor, Alfred Duff
Cooper, Leslie Hore-Belisha, Harold Macmillan, and Lord
Winterton, have voted against Chamberlain's policy. The
announcement of the figures is received by loud cries of
"Resign!" and "For God's sake, go!"

On May 10th, Clement Attlee and Arthur Greenwood
are called to Downing Street to be consulted on the prospect of Labour's co-operation. They refuse to serve under
Chamberlain, who at length is compelled to bow to the
gathering storm and resign his office in favour of Winston
Churchill. A new government comes into power at Westminster, and is faced, on the very day of Churchill's appointment, with a series of calamities such as no British
government has confronted throughout the long tale of
English history. Before breakfast on May 10th, Robert
accompanies our early morning tea with the announcement that we have dreaded for so long: "The Germans
have invaded Holland and Belgium! I've just heard it on
the wireless."

In five days, Holland has been overrun; in ten, the
French line is broken, and Weygand replaces Gamelin as
Commander-in-Chief. Persistent rumours that Gamelin has
committed suicide join a host of others, equally false. But
without the distracting interpolations of rumour, we know
now that, for the time being, the forces of cruelty and hatred
are dominant in Western Europe. The physical havoc ramp-

ant across the Channel is matched everywhere by the spiritual havoc of war—its bitterness and blind vituperation, its swift, demoralising eclipse of peacetime's noblest values. Like the countries of Europe going down before the invader, we confront the two greatest tragedies which history offers to a people. We face the ruin of those private worlds which hold all the warmth and sweetness of our existence; we contemplate the loss of our sons, the shattering of our homes, the ruthless termination of maturer lives which walked with death a quarter of a century ago. But, hardest of all, we who are part of England's faith in honesty and toleration must help to maintain her courage and idealism in a darkened world where the spiritual forces of love and truth are themselves the earliest casualties.

As the guns thunder across the Channel, Winston Churchill offers his supporters the sole reward of "blood and toil and tears and sweat." They are brave words, likely to echo permanently through the corridors of time. But the blood and the toil, the tears and the sweat, are actually being contributed by "Class 1940," which Will Dyson, in his famous prophetic cartoon drawn for the *Daily Herald* in 1919, perceived as a child crying behind a pillar while Clemenceau and his fellow-assassins of peace emerged from their job of treaty-making.

"In war," Arthur Greenwood tells the Labour Party Conference at Bournemouth, "there is no such thing as equality of sacrifice. Nothing man can offer weighs beside human life."

It is not the elderly politicians, but the young soldiers, whose blood is shed for the crass blunders made by the Old Men during the lost years in which peace might still have been guaranteed. Youth, and at present youth only, pays the price of such a conflict as this. Only when the summer is well advanced will civilian groups who have not, hitherto, met the direct cost of war, contribute their quota of casualties—the men past their prime, the wives and mothers, the children born through no fault of their own into a grievous era of peril and pain.

Amid the leisurely, incongruous luxuries of Bournemouth during Whit-week end, the annual Labour Party Conference finds that it has met chiefly to discuss and endorse the acceptance by Labour of a share in the new National Government. In the spacious rooms of the Highcliffe Hotel or beneath the coloured awnings of swing chairs on the garden terrace above the cliffs, Labour's representatives discuss the situation. Three or four times a day, the B.B.C. broadcast begins with gruesome tales of Europe's old centres of culture being overwhelmed by Nazi tanks, bombs, and parachutists, and ends with the news of Labour leaders appointed Ministers of the Crown. Rotterdam, where 30,000 people are killed in half an hour, crashes in a horror of burst water-mains and demolished dockside houses; Clement Attlee and Arthur Greenwood are invited to join the British War Cabinet. Those members of the Labour Party Executive who expect ministerial posts but have not yet been appointed, wander self-consciously round the comfortable lounges of the hotel, waiting for the broadcast which will mention them personally. At a mass meeting in Bournemouth Pavilion, Hugh Dalton, Ellen Wilkinson, and one or two of their colleagues explain, to the vehement satisfaction of an audience which is at least as interested in the sensational fact that Labour is returning to office as in its potential contribution to the conduct of the war, the responsible part which the Socialist leaders will play in the new administration. Ellen's brilliant speech, fiery as her flaming hair, makes doubly certain her chance of being included amongst those invited to serve.

Outside the Highcliffe Hotel, the warm early sunshine of a spring and summer so brilliant that few can remember its equal, bathes the South Coast in golden light. Bournemouth, like other seaside towns, has never appeared so beautiful. Her cliffs shine luminously white above a shimmering sea; from a distance the famous public rock-gardens resemble a patchwork quilt of orange and purple, scarlet and pink. In every wide sunny road, the sweet dry scent of innumerable fir-trees fills the air. As the party members sit on the terrace discussing political appointments, it is unbelievable that only a few miles away, across the misty blue sea which looks so serene below the yellow hedge of gorse that fringes the cliffs, men are destroying one another in their thousands, and the civilisation of half a dozen countries is going up in smoke and flame.

During the next few days, the beauty of England increases as the news gets steadily worse. Back again from Bournemouth, Martin and I walk round Kensington Gardens, now at their best, and find the Dutch garden—a glorified version of so many little gardens in Holland which have recently been ruined—radiant with crimson tulips and purple iris.

"Everyone, simple or subtle of mind," philosophises a *Times* editorial, "has been struck by the coincidence that the first stage of the war—the Sitzkrieg, as some call it—should have begun in an autumn of exceptional beauty, full of that rare harmony and lustre which Shelley discerned in the season, and that the 'total war,' the attempted Blitzkrieg, should start in an equally beautiful early summer."

He goes on to describe the urban loveliness which we have all observed, and now admire with the grim consciousness that any one of us may not be here to admire them much longer; the sequence of cherry, crab-apples, prunus and lilacs, followed by laburnum, May-trees and chestnuts, with the superb array of tulips always blooming beneath.

"If," he concludes, "the proposal to wipe London off the map has induced any sparing of flowers in her garden beds, the effect is not plain to the eye. . . . A long memory of London parks and gardens might be searched in vain for an early summer so beautiful as that of this fateful year."

Hour after hour, the news becomes graver as the "Battle of the Bulge" develops round Sedan. Constant B.B.C. exhortations to refrain from listening to rumours of a German break-through and a possible Allied defeat, suggest that these rumours have foundation in fact. This impression is confirmed when every day, before the early morning broadcast, lugubrious prayers for courage and a little hortative sermon in a Scottish accent indicate that we must now nerve ourselves to face unspeakable disasters. On May 19th Winston Churchill, less cautious, owing to an hereditary belief in British stamina, than the discreet B.B.C. announcers in acquainting us with the fate which looms before us, insists in a broadcast talk that the intensive warfare from which other countries have suffered will be upon us as soon as the situation has "stabilised" in France.

Again, as in the autumn, Martin and I, like other London householders, take the pictures off the walls, store our valuables in the basement, put buckets of sand in the passages, keep the bath filled with water, and make similar preparations, now universal, for fighting fires and minimising the effect of bombs. This done, I visit the hair-dresser, deciding that if I must be bombed, I may as well be bombed with neatly arranged hair.

We realise now that not London only, but all England, is in the first line of defence. The front is no distant battlefield to which a small contingent of men and women go forth, leaving family and friends with the sense that they have departed to some remote unimaginable adventure. To-day the front line is part of our daily lives; its dugouts and first-aid posts are in every street; its trenches and encampments occupy sections of every city park and every village green. Not only regiments, air squadrons, and the crews of ships are holding that line, but the whole nation, its families, households, and workers, whether they like it or not. Neither their talents nor their preferences have been consulted by the fate which is upon them.

Few of them do like it, but most are prepared to endure it. Even the minority which regards war as a crime and opposed this one to the moment of its outbreak, has no desire to run away. Its members prefer to remain and share their country's fortunes; to assume the responsibility for these all the more when for a time they happen to be adverse; to perform the outstanding duties of detached thought and humanitarian co-operation; to serve, not war, but their fellow men.

6. MEMORIAL SERVICE FOR CIVILISATION

On May 23, 1940, an impressive memorial service is held in Westminster Abbey. Waiting silently in the pale light that filters through the tall mullioned windows, hundreds of humble East Enders and obscure workers from peace organisations have gathered in this historic place to pay their last tribute to an old friend.

Two days before the full fury of the Blitzkrieg bursts over Europe, George Lansbury, once leader of the Labour Opposition in the House of Commons, passes into history. The most benevolent amongst First Commissioners of Works who created Lidos for the people of London, and the best beloved pacifist of his generation, he had written to a friend soon after his eightieth birthday: "I would love to close my life in freedom from strife, but if we are to save civilisation, we must still take part in the great crusade based on the eternal truth that man-made evils can by man be remedied."

While the Nazi war machine rolls over Holland and Belgium, "Uncle George's" body lies in state amid a glory of spring flowers in the drawing-room of his pleasant cottage in the wide Bow Road. Those friends who go down to the East End of London to bid him farewell realise that the nineteenth century, with its optimistic

Liberalism and its expanding horizons, has died with him. They are glad that he has not survived to witness, in widespread havoc and devastation, the material consequences of the breakdown of that international fellowship which he laboured to build. The sculptured features of his dead face, calm with the beautiful placidity of old age finally at rest, seem the last assurance of peace left in this world.

The new series of Nazi invasions has produced a rising clamour against unpopular minorities throughout England; both government and people are temporarily seized by a panic of suspicion from which they will be relatively free during the Battle for Britain. On the day preceding the memorial service—the Allies' "Black Tuesday"—the Germans have reached Boulogne, the House of Commons has introduced a Bill to punish spies and traitors with death, and Dr. C. E. M. Joad, who proposed the motion "This House will not fight for King and Country" at the Oxford Union in 1933, has published in the *News Chronicle a* recantation of his pacifism and a statement that nothing now matters but victory.

But the Right Honourable George Lansbury's venerable reputation is too secure to be impaired by the sudden national pursuit after Quislings and Fifth Columnists. Cabinet Ministers and Members of Parliament come to the Abbey; even the Prime Minister is represented by his dynamic red-haired secretary, Mr. Brendan Bracken. In a world of nations crying hatred and destruction on their brothers, the familiar lesson from I Corinthians 13 sounds strange with its insistence that charity never faileth and without it we are as sounding brass or a tinkling cymbal. Some of the men and women who listen half-consciously for the distant sound of guns across the Channel feel that this memorial service is held not for George Lansbury alone, but for European civilisation suicidally destroying itself and now unable to arrest the tide of fearful slaughter.

With pale, strained faces and throats half closed by rising emotions, the congregation cries to its God of Mercy in the all too appropriate final verse of the only hymn:

> Lord, by the stripes which wounded Thee,
> From death's dread sting Thy servants free,
> That we may live, and sing to Thee,
> Alleluya!

On the same day and at the same hour, a very different ceremony is taking place in another part of London. At Bow Street Police Court, six of George Lansbury's colleagues from the pacifist Peace Pledge Union, which he and the late Canon H. R. L. Sheppard founded in 1936, have been summoned to appear before Sir Robert Dummett, the Metropolitan Police Magistrate, for the second hearing of an official prosecution by the Attorney General. While the organ at Westminster Abbey thunders into the final crashing challenge of Blake's "Jerusalem," the six defendants stand in the dock beneath the lighted circular globes which hang from the white ceiling of the brown-panelled court, and confront the Attorney General, Sir Donald Somervell, K.C., who is leading the case for the prosecution. All of them Christian pacifists by profession or in spirit—"reputable citizens," reluctantly admits the magistrate, "though some people might call them wrong-headed"—they are perhaps subconsciously strengthened by the words of the anthem which the Westminster choir has just sung in Lansbury's memory:

I will lift up mine eyes unto the hills, from whence cometh my help. My help cometh even from the Lord, who hath made heaven and earth.

The hearing of this case, which comes to be popularly known as the Poster Trial, does not conclude until June 6th. In the official records of the Court, it is described as "The Police v. Alexander Wood, Maurice Rowntree, Stuart Morris, John Barclay, Ronald Smith and Sidney Todd." The first four defendants are respectively the chairman, treasurer, secretary, and group organiser of a pacifist body which includes 1,000 groups and 140,000 members; the two last are local group leaders at Forest Hills and Banbury. Their joint offence is the publication and exhibition of a poster displaying the words: "War will cease when men refuse to fight. What are YOU going to do about it?" Instead of attending the national memorial service for their old friend and leader, the six defendants appear at Bow Street during some of the most critical hours in their country's history to answer the following "said injunction":

Information has been laid this day by the Director of Public Prosecutions for that you between 1st February, 1940, and the 26th day of April, 1940, at 6 Endsleigh Street, W.C. 1 within the District aforesaid, did endeavour to cause among persons in His Majesty's Service Disaffection likely to lead to breaches of their duty, Contrary to Regulation 39a (1) (a) of the Defence (Ground) Regulations.

The Press publicity which would otherwise be given to this dramatic test of democratic rights in wartime, is eclipsed by the successive calamities of these disastrous weeks. While the British Expeditionary Force is heroically rescued from Dunkirk by coastal pleasure steamers, and the Third Republic of France is tottering towards its earth-shaking collapse, few newspapers have space to spare for the stubborn defence of their constitutional privileges put up by the representatives of a minority which must inevitably endure ostracism and persecution when war is raging. Actually, the result of the trial is one deeply significant to every democracy, for it establishes the principle, later embodied in a Memorandum issued by the Home Secretary on July 26, 1940, that "in this country no person should be penalised for the mere holding of an opinion, however unpopular that opinion may be to the majority."

From the outbreak of the war, the British pacifist movement has been exposed not only to normal criticism, but to a form of misrepresentation which tends sometimes to identify it with pro-Nazi sentiments, sometimes with the totally different war-resistance of the Communist Party. Most of its critics have failed to understand that the members of the Peace Pledge Union, the Fellowship of Reconciliation, and other less uncompromising peace societies are not so much opposed to war against Hitler, as to all war as an evil which can be avoided if sufficient national thought and will goes into the process. The majority are progressive liberals and socialists who detest Fascism and its methods as vehemently as anyone, but who suspect the popular argument (advanced during every war period) that war as a whole is wrong, but *this* war is the outstanding exception.

The members of the pacifist minority have arrived at their opinions by a variety of routes. Some hold a strong moral objection to the destruction of human life, maintaining that though a man should be ready to die for his country, he is not entitled to kill for it. Others are moved by the political consideration that war seldom attains its advertised objectives, and if undertaken against Nazism is less likely to lead to its annihilation than to the growth of totalitarianism in every country involved. But the largest number are pacifists on religious grounds. They believe war to be incompatible with the principles of Christianity as laid down in the Sermon on the Mount, and refuse to accept the compromise position of the Church of England. Pacifism to them means a way of life, involving the acceptance of certain values which Christ and other religious teachers have preached, but which organised Christianity has seldom practised.

"I hold my pacifism as part of my Christian faith," states Stuart Morris in evidence, after explaining that he has resigned his position as Canon of Birmingham Cathedral because he cannot accept the official attitude of the Church. "As I believe I am by vocation a preacher, I cannot recognise any limit to the range of the Gospel which I have to preach."

This heterogeneous group of political reformers and religious crusaders use various types of propaganda to disseminate their views. The one method which they neither approve nor have ever specifically attempted is the creation of disaffection among men serving in the Army, Navy, or Air Force. Though the allegation that the six defendants have endeavoured to create disaffection is the cause of their prosecution, the case as tried establishes the fact that the offending poster was actually issued two years before the outbreak of war. According to the evidence of Dr. Alexander Wood, a distinguished Fellow and Tutor of Emmanuel College, Cambridge, "that poster was part of the perfectly general public witness to the convictions which the pacifist movement holds. It was intended to be a challenge to everybody. It was neither primarily nor specifically directed to the Army. . . . I have two sons-in-law in the Army, and if I were going to start promoting disaffection, I should be inclined to start it nearer home. But I respect the decision that they have made."

Long before the trial has ended, it becomes clear that the Attorney General does not wish to press the case for the police. In giving judgment, the Chief Magistrate maintains that the failure to withdraw the poster is an infringement of the present defence regulations, but he merely binds over the defendants under the Probation of Offenders Act after they have undertaken that the poster will be discontinued owing to its liability to misinterpretation in time of war. This technical sentence is less significant than the arguments of the young defending counsel, Mr. J. F. F. Platts Mills, who is taking his last case before joining the Air Force, and their acceptance by the magistrate in spite of his obvious objection to the opinions of the defendants.

"Those views," quotes Mr. Platts Mills from a recent decision by Mr. Justice Stable, "which are only held by a few, which are unpopular, and which run counter to the great majority of the views of mankind, particularly in times of emotional crisis, as in times of war, are views which this Court is particularly jealous to preserve."

From his carved chair between two bookcases filled with leather-bound legal volumes, the old magistrate grimly agrees. Much as he dislikes the minority which the defendants represent, he has already admitted that "no one could imagine that any of you would give up the beliefs of a lifetime because of the present situation."

Now, while the Nazis occupy the Channel ports, and already, during the previous night, a series of coastal air-raids on England has begun, he dismisses the case in words that uphold the long tradition for which Cromwell wielded his sword and Milton his pen:

"This is a free country. We are fighting to keep it a free country, as I understand it, and these gentlemen, fortunately for them, in my judgment, are living in a country where they can express their pacifism, or their non-pacifism, with perfect freedom. They ought to be grateful to the men who are sacrificing their lives to preserve that right."

7. ENGLAND'S HOUR

ALL OVER EUROPE the Blitzkrieg is now at its height, destroying cities, towns, villages, and works of art which the men and women of the past created with infinite care; killing with bombs and machine-guns the men and women of to-day who would have been creators in their turn.

In London, barricades and heaps of sandbags are everywhere; barbed-wire entanglements and machine-gun emplacements transform familiar streets dominated for centuries by peace and prosperity. Occasional visits to the New Forest and the deceptive peace of the lovely spring countryside convey to us by comparison the extremity of the tension in London. The peace of the country is none the less purely relative; amid the rhododendrons and white may of Southern England are concealed searchlights, anti-aircraft guns, and ammunition dumps. In every town both large and small, anti-parachute corps (first known as "Parashots," then as "Local Defence Volunteers," and finally as "The Home Guards") are in process of formation.

The news from the Continent continues to be grave and obscure, but by the end of May it is obvious that the whole Maginot system has collapsed, and the Germans have pushed through from Sedan to Boulogne in only four days. In America the British Ambassador and Mr. Cordell Hull are already discussing a project by which the United States will receive thousands of children from an island kingdom facing invasion. On May 28th the Belgian king capitulates, thereby leaving open to the Nazis the road to Dunkirk through which supplies had gone to the British Army.

The loss of the British Expeditionary Force in France with all its equipment now begins to seem inevitable. In a short statement to the House of Commons, Winston Churchill urges Members to "suspend judgment," but warns them that "hard and heavy tidings" are likely to come to them within the next few days. The evacuation of the Army is its sole chance of escape, but can this be achieved? Invasion now seems certain, and the Ministry of Transport orders signposts to be removed from all roads lest they should guide descending parachutists. For a few days country towns are filled with stranded motorists whose identity cards passers-by, asked for directions, insist upon inspecting.

On the last day of May, Martin and I walk in Regent's Park amid shaded mauve pansies and pale pink lupines.

"It's just like a Sunday," I remark to him, for the Park is so deserted that it suggests a hot summer holiday when everyone who possesses something on wheels has gone into the country. Since most of the iron railings have now been removed from London's parks and squares for conversion into armaments, Regent's Park resembled a vast green field, very fresh and vivid. A few elderly people are sitting in chairs, a few young ones sailing in boats with striped sails. Again, as in the New Forest, comes the strange illusion of peace, due largely to the beauty of the summer and its scents and sounds. We feel as though we are watching the funeral of European civilisation elegantly conducted. Just so the Roman Empire must have appeared before the barbarians marched in.

Meanwhile, the evacuation of the British Expeditionary Force is beginning from Dunkirk. Under bombs and guns, men are carried across the Channel, not only by troopships, but by private yachts, river tugs, harbour lifeboats and coastal pleasure steamers—the "Saucy Sallies" of the summer season. The rescuers are not wholly male.

"Blast my sex!" cries a girl who offers her private yacht, to be told that men alone are eligible. The powers-that-be turn a blind eye in her direction and suspect that she finds her way to Dunkirk. Tired, half-clad, often with their clothes soaked through having to wade out to the rescuing steamers, the Army return. More heroism and more ingenuity are exercised over this haphazard evacuation than over any other in the history of the world. If the peace of Europe had been sought with half this energy, war would have been eliminated ten or more years ago. A batch of the rescued, marching through Waterloo station, are cheered until the glass roof rings with the sound.

I make one of my occasional visits to Bournemouth; the pleasant, clean-looking town is full of tattered French and Belgian soldiers, with an occasional red Moroccan fez amongst them. For a moment I dream that I am back in that most cosmopolitan of ports, Valetta, during a period of Mediterranean war service in 1917; but Valetta smelt strongly of monks and goats, while Bournemouth radiates the warm scent of firs and cut grass. In the public gardens a little plump English boy scrambles backwards and forwards over two recumbent French soldiers, who obviously enjoy the game.

That night, Winston Churchill announces that over 300,000 of the British Expeditionary Force have been saved, and the Ministry of Home Security, with an eye on the future, decrees that no camping is to be allowed within ten miles of the coast in the East and South of Britain.

On June 5th we learn of a great new German thrust towards Paris, the next objective before our own turn comes. In the midst of it, we go down to Swanage for Hilary's half-term.

"At least we shall get three quiet nights here," I say to Martin, for our week-ends at the cottage near Southampton are already disturbed by gunfire and distant explosive thuds. I have hardly fallen asleep when a terrific explosion—the fall of a heavy bomb—awakens me, and through the attic window on the top floor of the small country hotel, I see a searchlight vividly streaking the sky. There is an outburst of conversation; one or two visitors run wildly up and down the stairs.

"Where's it fallen?"

"It must be the Isle of Wight!"

"No—it sounded more like Bournemouth."

When Hilary's school play is over next evening, Martin and I stroll round the headland beyond the hotel, and remark on the strange unreality of the lovely landscape which conveys so false an impression of tranquillity. I remember the same sensation during the last war, when in the summer of 1918 I watched the mirage-like camouflaged trawlers slip past the Cornish coast, and feel that the life of my generation is like a recurring decimal in which the grimmest of experiences are repeated again and again. From an army acquaintance whom we meet in the town, we learn that, deposited beneath the ancient and now disused pier which so innocently spans one corner of the bay, lies a sufficient quantity of gelignite to blow it up on the spot.

All through the blazing southern heat of that June week-end, the Germans are pressing the French back towards Paris in spite of tank-traps and barricades. Hilary's headmaster is already discussing the possibility of transferring his coeducational school to Canada; Swanage, he thinks, must soon be declared a defence area, and it will be pointless to remove the school to some new district of this small island when every remote corner is now accessible to bombs. We say goodbye to Hilary at the school gate, and turn to watch her walking up the hill with her gas-mask in one hand and the toy animals we have bought her in the other—a stalwart, self-possessed little figure in a red and white check frock.

"Such an effort," I think, in spite of myself, "to bring a child through its first ten years of life—and now, for what?"

In London we learn that the Germans have reached Beauvais on the road to Paris; the next day Italy enters the war in time to stake a claim to the spoils. At midnight President Roosevelt broadcasts from the University of Virginia, describing his efforts to keep Italy out of the war by negotiation, and pledging the resources of the United States to the help of the Allies. All the time he is speaking, the Nazis cut in on the radio with broadcasts of their national anthem and the Horst Wessel Song. During the next three days, the Germans press down on Paris, the Bourse and several ministries move into the provinces, and a steady stream of refugees, finally reaching several million, leaves Paris and blocks the main roads for thirty miles to the south. On the wireless, a project is discussed for evacuating British children in thousands to the Dominions. Princess Juliana of Holland, we learn, and her two baby daughters are already in Canada.

Five days later, as we leave for Richard's half-term at Malvern, it is announced that church and chapel bells are now to be rung only as a warning of the approach of air-borne troops. At Paddington station, the early evening newspapers are already predicting the capture of Paris; by the time we reach our destination, the great city has fallen in a thunderous collapse which will echo through history to the end of time.

As we enter the Herefordshire village inn where we usually stay for Richard's half-term week-ends, the French-born wife of the proprietor greets us with tears.

"My family," she cries, "my family in Paris! Your nation 'has let us down!"

We feel that the accusation might be reversed, but sympathetically refrain from mentioning Dunkirk or the bridges over the Meuse.

On Saturday, June 15th, the swastika flies from the Eiffel Tower, and the *Daily Mail* publishes the outline of an American scheme for sending a hundred thousand British children to the United States. From the top of the Priory Church at Malvern, Richard and I look at the beautiful English landscape stretching from Worcester to Wells. How will this still untouched country appear when the German bombers have visited it? I ask myself silently, as Walter de la Mare's too poignant line echoes through my mind:

Look thy last on all things lovely . . .

We take Richard to the afternoon cinema; we have left the gas-masks necessary for admission at our hotel, but get in by deceitfully purchasing containers and stuffing them with paper. After we have watched a long escapist film displaying the antics of the Marx Brothers, a picture showing the London docks concludes the programme. I can hardly bear to watch it, wondering what the next phase of the war will do to those crowded acres of active humanity and essential stores. That night the local evening paper, though full of sinister information, denies that France will conclude a separate peace; but before the week-end is over, the Pétain government has taken office and is preparing to do so.

On June 18th, when we are back in London, Winston Churchill makes one of the historic speeches of this war. As usual the weather is hot and brilliant; as I wait in the Central Lobby of the House of Commons, the high stained-glass windows stand open, showing the fairylike fabric of carved stone in clear golden sunshine.

"We're in the biggest mess since the Battle of Hastings," remarks a Welsh M.P. with realistic pessimism. I notice how the coloured reflections from the windows fall upon the sculptured shoulders of former statesmen, not one of whom was confronted with a situation remotely comparable to the present crisis.

Big Ben strikes four as solemnly as though it is announcing the hour of doom, and Winston Churchill begins his speech—a speech in the heroic warrior tradition of his ancestors, to whom the sanity of peaceful mediation was an undesirable form of compromise. He speaks of the colossal disaster of the collapse of France and the futility of recrimination, since, "if we open a quarrel between the past and the present, we shall find that we have lost the future." He reminds the Members of the House again that "the worst possibilities" are open, and once more records the resolve of Britain and the British Empire to fight on, "if necessary for years, if necessary alone." About the severity of the ordeal before them he speaks frankly, but, like every member of the class which has ruled England since the Norman Conquest and has repeatedly carried it into war, he expects the much-enduring British people to stand up to it "at least as well as any other people in the world."

Finally, the fire of his conclusion reflects his personal belief—not shared by all his countrymen, but entertained by him with dynamic fervour from the time that Nazidom came to power—in the necessity of the war to which England is committed.

"The battle of Britain is about to begin. Upon this battle depends the survival of Christian civilisation. Upon it depends our own British life and the long continuity of our institutions and our Empire. The whole fury and might of the enemy must very soon be turned on us. Hitler knows that he will have to break us in this island or lose the war. If we can stand up to him all Europe may be free, and the life of the world may move forward into broad sunlit uplands, but if we fail, then the whole world, including the United States, and all that we have known or cared for, will sink into the abyss of a new dark age made more sinister, and perhaps more prolonged, by the light of a perverted science. Let us therefore brace ourselves to our duty and so bear ourselves that if the British Commonwealth and Empire lasts for a thousand years, men will still say, 'This was their finest hour.' "

Two days later, the French plenipotentiaries have been received by the Germans, and David Low, the cartoonist, has published in the *Evening Standard* a drawing of a solitary soldier in a steel helmet, standing on Dover's cliffs and shaking his fist at the blazing vanquished Continent. The caption beneath the picture contains only three words: "Very well, alone!"

8. AND SO—FAREWELL!

Towards the end of June, many conscientious parents throughout England find themselves confronted with a heartbreaking dilemma.

Simultaneously with the collapse of France, the government announces an official scheme to send thousands of British children to the Dominions. Canada, South Africa, Australia, and New Zealand broadcast enthusiastic offers of hospitality. In the United States, a committee is formed under the chairmanship of Marshall Field of Chicago to rescue Europe's children; it is even possible, we learn, that the adamant immigration laws may be modified in order to admit a hundred thousand boys and girls of British stock to America.

We feel certain that the government would not sponsor so large a scheme unless it was convinced that horror and dislocation would come to this country with the downfall of Europe. The announcement of the plan seems to thousands of anxious parents a warning of "things to come." Earlier evacuation schemes have made no special appeal to them, for moving children from the town to the country was merely a method of redistributing the population; it assured neither safety, freedom from chaos, nor that sense of security which is the birthright of childhood. Emigration to the Dominions or America, where real free-

dom from war will be a gift from new territories un-
hampered by the evil nationalistic traditions of the quar-
relsome Old World, is a proposition more hopeful and
far more imaginative. The most resourceful and energetic
parents decide to register their children immediately.

From the moment that the Children's Overseas Reception Board—to be known familiarly as "Corb"—is established in the Berkeley Street offices of Messrs. Thomas
Cook & Son under the chairmanship of Geoffrey Shakespeare, Under-Secretary of State for the Dominions, a
queue of parents and children begins to stretch from the
office door into Piccadilly. The opportunity of safeguard-
ing the children's future appeals equally to the small
households of Mayfair and the large dockyard families
from Bermondsey and Chatham.

"If we must die," say these fathers and mothers, "at
least we intend to save the next generation."

Sick at heart, conscious that our obligations as parents
may demand a sacrifice of a kind we had never contemplated, Martin and I debate the question for a weary
week-end. Richard is at school in a so-called "safe area,"
but Hilary, at Swanage, has already been summoned to
the air-raid shelter; and her headmaster has finally con-
cluded that no place nearer than Canada can now offer
a stable life and an uninterrupted education. We ourselves
have lived in the United States, on and off, for fifteen
years; we have friends tested by a decade of loyal affection. Shall we not be sadly remiss as parents if we fail
to take advantage of circumstances so favourable?

"It's a terrible thing to do," I protest, unable, after
twelve years of careful rearing, to face giving up the
children just when their personalities are developing and
their fascination is growing every day.

"You're only thinking of yourself," Martin replies inexorably. "It's the children's interests that matter, not your feelings."

I agree with him miserably. "I know that. I'm only trying to decide whether it's better for them to have danger with me or security without me. As you feel so certain, you're probably right."

After one more night of agonized indecision, I accompany Martin to the offices of the Children's Overseas Reception Board. Two humble units in a long line of troubled questioning parents, we make our inquiries. The woman Member of Parliament who answers them happens to be a personal friend.

"Don't hesitate," she advises us. *"Get them out!"*

She hands us several alternative application forms; one is a request for permission to make private arrangements without waiting for the government scheme to come into operation.

"Look here," she adds, "you could afford to pay for their passage, couldn't you?"

We admit that we could. "The children have been to the United States before," we continue. "They both hold re-entry permits."

"Well, then, there's nothing to wait for. They're in quite an exceptionally favourable position. Fix up their passages yourselves, and you'll be making room under the government scheme for two more children whose parents can't afford to send them on their own."

We decide to take her advice and book provisional berths for Richard and Hilary, never dreaming that in three weeks' time, when the operation of the government scheme has been impeded by the loss of the French fleet and the resulting shortage of convoys, we and other middle-class parents who have acted with similar promptitude will have our distress increased by accusations that we have abused our "class privileges" at the expense of children from state-aided schools whose interests under the scheme we believed ourselves to be serving.

When we visit the Passport Office to obtain passports for Richard and Hilary, there is certainly no evidence that the queue of parents which stretches to the end of Dartmouth Street is composed of "wealthy escapists." For over an hour we stand waiting in the company of a former army corporal, who is using his savings to send his family to a Canadian sergeant whom he knew in World War No. 1.

"Yes," he explains, "I'm sending the wife and kid. She don't want to go, but I tells her: 'You mark my words, it'll be the only life, after this war. The boy won't 'ave 'arf a chance here, compared with over there. When it's all over,' I says to her, 'I'll come out and join you.' "

At last we are inside the Passport Office, where another waiting line stretches down a long passage. After standing, without lunch, for nearly three hours, we finally receive the necessary forms, and file our applications with the names of the children's kindly guarantors. No less than four friends, with the uncalculating generosity of hospitable America, have offered them a home—two members of my publishing firm; the principal of a famous girls' school in Dallas, Texas; and a child specialist from St. Paul, Minnesota, and his gifted wife, with whom I have three times stayed. It is to these last that we have decided to send our children for the present, and in order that they may land as near as possible to their destination, we have applied for their passage on a Canadian Pacific liner sailing a few days hence.

On Monday, Martin returns to the Passport Office, and finds that the children's papers are ready. After several visits to Cook's and the office of the Canadian Pacific Line, their berths are finally allocated. Except to their boarding schools supervised by masters or mistresses, they have never travelled without me before, but now they must go as "unaccompanied children" in the care of an unknown stewardess, taking their chance with ninety others similarly situated if an "emergency" should arise.

Again that night, as I am going to bed, I feel that I cannot face this separation; cannot endure to submit Richard and Hilary for one terrible week to the intensive danger of torpedoes in order that they may be removed from the long-drawn risk of bombs and economic dislocation. I have work to do, and cannot accompany them: how shall I confront the suspense of that week? Even though I do not yet know that, while my son and daughter are on the ocean, the *Arandora Star* will be sunk five days before I learn that they are safe and well, I cannot find within me sufficient strength and courage to let them go in such circumstances as these. Late that evening, I have arrived at so fierce a stage of desperation that the sudden wail of the air-raid siren over midnight London comes as an unexpected relief. It is the first time that we have heard it in town for many months, and though no raid comes to our district the threat pulls me together with its reminder of the ordeal before this country.

The next day, the children are to return from their schools. All the arrangements have been completed, but with only twenty-four hours to spare, any last-minute hitch will destroy the whole plan. Their lives, and perhaps their entire future, may depend on the punctual catching of a train and its safe arrival.

Hilary is due first, and we meet her at Waterloo. She seems undisturbed by her impending emigration, and is interested only in relating her recent adventures.

"We were in the air-raid shelter for *three* hours last night," she tells me triumphantly. "And we were there for two the night before! Susie said she saw a German bomber brought down!"

I examine her carefully, but as yet her little sunburned face shows no trace of fatigue. How soon, I speculate, would the shadows have come under her eyes? How quickly would those interrupted nights have ceased to appear adventurous? Two hours later, Richard arrives at Paddington. In his safer area he has heard no alarms, but he accepts our decision with the philosophic stoicism of twelve years old.

"It's all right," he confides, "so long as Hilary's going to America too!"

"Then you don't mind Daddy and me not coming with you?"

"Oh, no! It's half the fun, being by ourselves."

The children have brought their hastily packed school trunks with them. It is already tea-time; I have only two hours in which to re-pack for both before I help them to get to bed. All the necessary clothes that I can lay hands on go in first; then, with a sudden overwhelming nausea, I pack their personal treasures—Richard's stamp collection and Hilary's private zoo. How long before I see those cherished possessions again? Six months? Two years? A lifetime?

"O God, I cannot bear it!"

Whose voice was that? Surely not mine! Yet swift as thought, from nowhere, comes the reply.

"You've got to bear it. This is War. You know already from your own experience that war takes the dearest human relationships and tramples them ruthlessly into the dust. It has no concern for love and marriage, for maternity and childhood. If you want to save your children, you must pay its price."

The morning so long dreaded has come. Last night I delayed as long as I could over drying Hilary's slim fairy-like body and brushing Richard's thick nut-brown hair. Sleepless, I looked at their sleeping faces—Richard's long dark eyelashes motionless on his cheeks, Hilary's fair serene face as unperturbed as an angel's. Modern children, endowed as though by some law of compensation with a calm emotional detachment which they cannot have inherited from their war-ridden parents of the Lost Generation, they neither fear nor even speculate about the adventure before them.

We join the waiting boat train at Euston, our luggage-laden taxicab hemmed in a long cavalcade of vehicles which threads its way laboriously through the newly barricaded entrance to the station. Just in time we board the train and discover that it is crowded with children—children of both sexes and all ages, babies whose fortunate mothers are justified in leaving an invasion-threatened country and going with them, older children who vary from five or six years old to the school ages of fourteen and fifteen. Most of them are being accompanied to the boat by their parents—miserable mothers and fathers of whom some are even now torn cruelly with indecision. On the way back to London we are to meet an unhappy father whose departing wife, right up to the moment of embarkation, announced her intention of returning to London with her boy and girl.

Like the rest of the children in the train, Richard and Hilary remain philosophical, even with regard to the dangers that they may encounter on the way to Montreal.

"Wonder if we'll meet any submarines?" speculates Richard, voicing with no inhibition of fear the secret dread that tears at our hearts, challenging our resolution, making us perpetually uncertain whether we have acted for the best. It is the parents, not the children, who are suffering; at least we can thank God for that. As the crowded train rolls inexorably onwards, the hackneyed verse of a familiar hymn seems to beat into my brain with the roar of the wheels.

> If Thou shouldst ask me to resign
> What most I prize, it ne'er was mine.
> I only yield Thee what is Thine.
> Thy Will be done!

At the docks we are ushered into a large covered shed, to wait for what seem infinite hours till the immigration officials arrive. Tired out already by the long train journey, the dozens of babies lift their voices one by one in loud wails of protest, and soon the dock resembles the parrot-house at the Zoo. Looking up and down the huge enclosure at two or three hundred weary older children sitting with mute resignation beside their suitcases, we conclude that the immigration officials cannot be fathers. At least a number of stewardesses take pity on the waiting families; they bring cartons of milk and packets of biscuits, which they offer to children and parents. Martin and I feel that the biscuits would choke us, but Richard and Hilary, seizing their supply with eager grubby hands, both cheerfully consume eight biscuits and two cartons of milk.

A Canadian Pacific official approaches us.

"Are these the children who hold re-entry permits to the United States?"

Richard and Hilary move forward in proud assent. Now that the moment has come, my legs suddenly feel as though they will no longer sustain me. Oh, my darling children, is there time to call you back from salvation, even now?

With imperturbable dignity, Richard and Hilary march off beside the C.P.R. official into the hut where the immigration officers are sitting. As we watch them from a distance, we notice a long file of girls from a Yorkshire convent school move towards the gangway, accompanied by their gentle nuns. Are these the wealthy, taking advantage of their privileges? They exist, perhaps, on other liners; not many of them seem to be boarding this one.

Apparently without a qualm, the children exhibit their papers and their money. After answering several questions, they reappear with their escort.

"The only thing that worried me," Richard confesses, "was whether they'd let me keep the five shillings Granny gave me, as well as my ten pounds."

"And did they, darling?"

"Yes," chimes in Hilary. "They didn't mind a bit. Richard said: 'Have I got to give you my five shillings, because I'm only supposed to take ten pounds?' and the man said: 'Never mind, sonny; we won't worry about that.'"

A cold rainy wind blows suddenly over the docks. Be-

yond the enclosure we see now the grey-painted hulk of
the anonymous liner, waiting to carry away from us the
dearest possessions that are ours on earth. No—not our
possessions. We never possessed them; they have always
possessed themselves.

The C.P.R. official approaches again. His manner is dis-
creetly sympathetic.

"I'm afraid you'll have to say goodbye to the children
now."

"Very well," we reply with outward equanimity. I remember then that I have brought no farewell gifts for
either, that I was packing throughout the two hours that
the children went shopping with their father. Oh, dearest
Richard and Hilary—will you think of me as the careless
mother who never gave you a parting present when you
bought her such a lovely bunch of scarlet carnations?

"Goodbye, Mummie! Goodbye, Daddy!"

"Goodbye, my own darlings. You'll look after Hilary,
won't you, Richard? And you, sweetheart—you *will* do
what Richard tells you on the boat?"

"We'll be quite all right, Mummie. Don't worry about
us. We promise we'll look after ourselves till you come
across too."

"Goodbye, then, my loves!" (*If Thou shouldst ask me
to resign What most I prize . . .*)

With the gallant pathetic courage of children, Richard
and Hilary kiss us and leave us as calmly as though they
are departing for a week-end visit to a familiar relative.
Their eyes are bright; their faces do not change as they
go with their guide to meet the unknown adventure.

At the entrance to the gangway, they turn and wave
cheerfully. Then the tarpaulin flaps behind them, and
they are gone.

9. CITY PARK

THE CITY PARK runs between the bridges, stretching a mile southward from the river bank. At sunset on summer evenings, the population of the working-class district on its southern boundary have always taken the air on the riverside path.

They take it still, but without their families. From the once green space beneath the trees where the children played, their perambulators, scooters and fairy cycles have vanished. Instead of mail-carts, the materials for completing the half-finished pontoon bridge across the river lie upon the muddy earth whence the grass has disappeared. On fine Sundays, the young men of the district use the ends of the bridge as diving boards. The huge planks and thick wooden stakes fill the warm midsummer air with the smell of damp wood. In its three bridges, two power stations, and one large gasometer, the area round the park has a fine collection of military objectives, but nobody now takes any notice of the sinister wooden pile or discusses its implications.

This morning, in the sunshine, one hundred Nazi aeroplanes have attacked the South-East coast. Above the city, the protecting barrage balloons hang low in the sky. When they go up, the city dwellers know that the "yel-

low signal" has been hoisted by order of the Air Ministry
to indicate the approach of raiders. The signal will only
become red if the raiders actually appear.

According to the angle from which you regard them,
these balloons resemble huge oxidised fish, or swollen pigs
with large distended ears. When they soar higher, they
take on the more romantic appearance of pearl beads float-
ing beneath the clouds. Sometimes, in sunshine, they recall
the admiring words of Oswald Garrison Villard, who
found them, during this war's first autumn, "as exquisite
when beneath blue skies as jewels in a rajah's raiment."

The centre of the park has always been covered by
several acres of original forest, which flourished when
half the modern city was still marshland, and its busy
commercial river a placid country stream. It is here, where
the undergrowth is battered and the grass grows long,
that the absence of gardeners called up for military service
becomes most evident. Beyond the wood, the great playing field where the city boys played Saturday cricket is
broken from end to end by a deep diametrical trench,
and covered at intervals with heaps of red-brown soil to
prevent the possible landing of hostile aeroplanes. Pressing inwards from the circumference of the field as further
acres of recreation ground are brought under cultivation,
the park allotments display a flourishing patriotic output
of cabbages, carrots, turnips and runner-beans.

Close to the road skirting the park lie the covered
trenches which will shelter the strolling population caught
by an air-raid. The velvet-smooth green where the old
men play bowls is surrounded with sand-heaps like the
cricket field, but the city grandfathers disregard them.
Not Hitler, Stalin and Mussolini combined can interfere
with the time-honoured attractions of their ancient game.
In the subtropical garden close to the green, the lawn

is still smoothly mown and the exotic flowers make a brave display of colour. Beneath the drooping heavy foliage of copper-beeches and sycamores, women with dogs on leather leads sit anxiously studying the newspapers instead of reading detective stories. Here, at last, one sees a few children. Many are evacuees whose parents have brought them back from the country with the excuse that one part of England is now hardly safer than another.

"Anyhow," say the mothers with fatalistic resignation, "it don't do no good goin' away if a bomb's got your name on it."

In the middle of a large gravelled enclosure, the covered bandstand shelters a tarpaulin-shrouded object which may be a piano or a small machine-gun. Round it, still incongruously grouped in rows, stand the green painted iron chairs where the music-loving population once sat to hear Gilbert and Sullivan or Handel's "Messiah." The railings which bounded the path leading to the bandstand have now been removed to make metal for munitions. Somewhere amid the heavy clusters of trees is concealed a searchlight which flashes above the river, a white pointing finger, when the Nazi aeroplanes are heard overhead. The bombers have a heavy, massive hum, quite different from the lighter, more casual-sounding British machines. All the difference between the Teutonic and Anglo-Saxon temperaments seems to lie in those two familiar noises.

The brick recreation hut close to the river has now been reinforced with sandbags, but the wireless music echoing from within has the same sentimental sweetness as before. On the broad top of the low wall, a young man in grey-blue Air Force uniform sits reading a novel as he listens to the gentle sound. Of all the park's many resources, only the artificial lake and the Old English garden remain unchanged.

In this little paved flower-garden, business—or rather pleasure—is going on as usual. "Rubbish must not be dumped here," warns the notice at the entrance—a gentle hint for Hitler's Fifth Columnists to convey to aerial intruders. The fountain is playing in the centre pond, covered with an exuberant growth of pink and white water-lilies which have responded generously to the fine warm summer. The scarlet and gold of dahlias, antirrhinums and pyrethrums burns from the flower-beds. Along the paved paths, the sparrows hop and peck as unconcernedly as they pecked twelve months ago. On the circular benches of grey seasoned wood, the old and the tired sit as placidly as they have sat for generations.

Undeterred by Europe's tragedy, the gardeners have started an innovation in the shape of a cactus bed. The prickly fleshy leaves bring back a January recollection of cactuses in the Arizona desert, but the wet, chocolate-coloured earth from which they spring bears no resemblance to the dry red soil of that summer land. A small middle-aged woman in black addresses one of the brown-uniformed gardeners.

"So you're still keeping up the garden in spite of the war?"

"Oh, yes," he answers. "We shall carry on if the air-raids don't stop us."

"But why should you close the garden because of air-raids?"

"Well," he surmises, "if the bombin' got too bad, people wouldn't have no 'eart to look at flowers."

"I don't know," meditates his questioner. "When things went wrong in the last war, looking at flowers was sometimes the only comfort I had. If you can't have safety, you seem to need beauty all the more."

10.   APPELLATE TRIBUNAL

THE LONG LIGHT room at the top of Ebury Bridge House, near Victoria station, bears little resemblance to a Court of Justice. Its white ceiling and light yellow walls give it the appearance of a very new classroom, with windows looking down upon Pimlico's tree tops and the roofs of London.

Behind a green cloth-covered table, the Appellate Tribunal for Conscientious Objectors sits gravely examining the cases before it. The Chairman, Lord Fleming, has taken the place of Mr. H. A. L. Fisher, Warden of New College, Oxford, who was killed in a street accident on his way to a session. His colleagues are Sir Cyril Norwood, formerly Headmaster of Harrow and now President of St. John's College, Oxford, and Sir Arthur Pugh, once a trade union organiser whose dapper appearance suggests that he ought to change places with the stalwart peer.

As I enter the room, a black-haired young man in a navy blue coat is appealing through his lawyer against the decision of his local Tribunal refusing him exemption to do agricultural work. Indiscreetly supported by a foolish and loquacious mother, he explains that he is already working on a small holding, and hopes to take up agriculture as a permanent occupation. To this intelligent but superficially educated boy, the members of the Tribunal put a series of questions which a student of history for twenty years would answer with reluctance.

"How do you distinguish," inquires one, "between this war and former wars?"

The young man answers slowly but with care:

"I do think civilians suffer more to-day. After all, they're just being murdered—and people in the past did know more what they were fighting about."

"Have you read much history? What about the Thirty Years' War? Surely the suffering of civilians to-day is not one tithe of what the Germans suffered then?"

The young man—not without better reason than he realises—looks dubious, and murmurs that he would find it difficult to discover a just war in history. His interrogators—in a manner which strangely combines toleration with severity—continue their questioning.

"So your doctrine is one of complete non-resistance?"

"Yes, it is."

"In the world as you would run it, then, the aggressor would always attain his ends?"

"I believe that non-violent resistance would have a great moral effect."

The Tribunal, which has obviously listened to much theorising about non-violent resistance, treats the subject with a scepticism which not even Gandhi could shake.

"Did the non-resistance of Denmark have a greater effect on the German people than the resistance of the Dutch?"

But the young man is not to be intimidated. He believes that hatred and anger produce anger and hatred, and says so with such persistence that his questioners finally abandon history and politics for inquiries about his small holding. From this subject they go on—as with every appellant —to put questions designed to unearth the origin of his conscientious objection to war. Those young pacifists who can give evidence that their opinions long antedated the present "emergency" fare better than converts of more recent duration. The would-be agriculturist—who states that he started to think when the international situation began to deteriorate—is obviously a problem to the learned trio behind the green cloth table. After consultation, they tell the boy that their decision is reserved and he will receive it by post.

Between 1914 and 1918, as in 1939 and 1940, there were many men of military age who devised ingenious methods of avoiding army service without challenging public opinion. Yet then, as now, it was the honest objectors, rather than the skin-saving type known to the Army as "skrimshankers," who incurred public odium for their views. Both the British governments of World War No. 2 have had wisdom enough to profit by the experience of World War No. 1, which proved that persecution even to the point of the shooting squad could not induce sincere objectors to change their minds. The verdict given at the Poster Trial has also had its effect. Though it received so little publicity, it has helped to maintain the official attitude of comparative toleration towards conscientious objectors which still contrasts favourably with that of the last war.

In those days the fighting Tommies who faced maximum danger often had greater sympathy for pacifist opinions than either their superior officers, or the civilians who sat in judgment without putting themselves to any comparable test. A distinguished member of the Society of Friends was serving a prison sentence for war resistance, when an attack of measles compelled the authorities to put him into the same hospital ward as a number of serving soldiers. Next morning the medical officer doing his rounds discovered the category of his new patient, and proceeded vehemently to state his opinion of conscientious objectors.

"What," he thundered, "would have happened in 1914 if everybody had behaved like you?"

As he turned his back and marched up the ward, the soldier occupying the next bed was heard to remark *sotto voce*: "Bloody fool! No bloody war, of course!"

Since the Military Tribunals of 1914–1918 were notoriously unsympathetic in their treatment of pacifists, the Chamberlain government set up fifteen civilian Tribunals to hear the arguments of conscientious objectors in different parts of England, and an Appellate Tribunal in London to which objectors who believed themselves to be the victims of unfair decisions could bring their cases as a last resort. In the Churchill government, that most truculent of fighters, Ernest Bevin, has consistently used his authority at the Ministry of Labour to defend the conscientious objectors accepted and officially registered by Tribunals against victimisation by local authorities. A Home Office Memorandum issued in July, 1940, by Sir John Anderson, not only stated that no person should be penalised for the mere holding of an opinion, but insisted that "mere membership of any organisation which has not been declared to be unlawful does not of itself afford any cause of action against a public servant."

From the outbreak of the war to June 27, 1940, the official total of conscientious objectors as given in the House of Commons was 43,534, or 1.4 per cent. of all

the men called to register for military service up to that
date. The present total is probably between 50,000 and
60,000. Of the men who have appeared before the Tribunals, 18 per cent. have received unconditional exemption. The largest number, 45 per cent., have been placed
in Category B (conditional exemption), which releases
them from military service on condition that they undertake work of national importance under civilian authorities. Of the remaining 37 per cent., 20 per cent. have been
removed from the category of conscientious objectors as
such and placed on the military register but only for non-
combatant service, while 17 per cent. have been refused
exemption but with the right of appeal. If the verdict of
the Appellate Tribunal confirms the original finding, these
applicants must choose between military service and im-
prisonment.

On this Friday morning in August, the Tribunal's exam-
inations continue. The case of the would-be land worker
is followed by that of a twenty-three-year-old plumber,
whose dumb nervousness gains him no alternative to the
decision of the local tribunal, which awarded him non-
combatant service. In quick succession follow an unemployed carpenter whose membership of the "Assemblies
of God" causes the local tribunal's decision to be reversed,
an estate agent who would only agree to non-combatant
duty if he could do it for both sides and whose case is
reserved, and an insurance agent who ruins his chances
from the start by referring to the duties of soldiers as
"dirty work." The sixth case—and the last of those that
I hear—is the most significant on the morning time-table,
for it is the evidence of the boy's mother which causes
the decision of the local tribunal to be changed. He

brings also another witness—the minister of his local Congregational church—who refuses to respond to Lord Fleming's cross-examination.

"Sir," he asserts with dignity, "it is not *my* views which are being challenged."

The Chairman turns to the young man.

"And what is your occupation, Mr. Maishman?"

"I'm working with the Thermostat Company in Sudbury."

"How long have you entertained your present views?"

"Since 1935. I became a pacifist after hearing Dick Sheppard and George Lansbury and Donald Soper speak at a Peace Pledge Union meeting. I joined the P.P.U. directly after, and I was just going to join the Fellowship of Reconciliation when conscription came in, and I was afraid it would seem as if I was doing it just to strengthen my case."

The Tribunal calls the boy's mother to give evidence. She is a quiet, self-contained woman with deep emotions which she keeps, wisely, under control.

"My boy was born four days after his father was killed in the last war," she says, and a listening silence falls upon the light room with its little group of applicants, witnesses and spectators.

"Have you any other children?"

"No, sir. He's my only one. I was bitter at first—felt nothing could be bad enough for the Germans. Then one day, when my baby was a year old, I suddenly began thinking: 'Perhaps there's a German woman just lost her husband who feels the same about me as I felt about her.' And I've been a pacifist ever since."

"Did you bring up your son to be a pacifist too?"

"Well, sir, I did take him to peace meetings. But I

didn't try to influence nis decision about this war. He's come to that on his own."

Like pacifists in general, about two-thirds of all conscientious objectors base their opposition to war on religious convictions. Most of them are sincere young men, anxious to serve their country in any humanitarian fashion that their fellows will accept. They are not objectors because they fear death; one—an air-raid warden—was killed through returning to his first-aid post in Portsmouth when the Blitzkrieg started, though he was officially off duty. Their objection is not to dying but to killing, and their chief problem, in a country where many factories are wholly or partly reorganised for munition-making, is the narrowing opportunity for rendering service in a fashion that their consciences can approve.

Many would acknowledge that, in such a war as this, pacifism for the time being is a lost cause which has no hope of triumphing or even of increasing its limited influence. But they would probably agree with the hero of the film "Mr. Smith Goes to Washington" that the lost causes are perhaps the only ones worth fighting for. If you ask them the source of their inspiration they will tell you that they live for the future, remembering that Christianity did not end with the crucifixion, nor the cause of slave-emancipation with the death of John Brown.

Meanwhile, their usefulness to their country is not ended because they cannot now effectively oppose the war or immediately sponsor a negotiated peace. Quite apart from the civilian services which many are rendering, and the maintenance of rational judgments and charitable values which is their special function, they have a definite task to perform in opposing the growth of totalitarianism wherever they find it. By insisting that there is always a Higher Authority than the State, they are helping to maintain an England which will still be in a position to restore the liberties that she has sacrificed when the war is over.

11. AREOPAGUS

It is August 4, 1940. Those of us who are old enough to remember World War No. 1 cannot help recalling that the day is the twenty-sixth anniversary of the explosion which shattered the tranquil, prosperous world of our childhood, and deprived our doomed generation—we now know for ever—of peace and normality.

How many, I wonder, of the people of England, now engulfed in World War No. 2, will notice the significance of this brilliant Sunday—one of the hottest and sultriest of our ironically perfect summer? I decide to go to Hyde Park, and spend the afternoon in listening to the week-end orators proclaiming their opinions.

I soon discover that, to the moving throng which covers the dry grassy spaces between Marble Arch and Hyde Park Corner, the day is not the twenty-sixth anniversary of the Great War, but the Sunday before the Monday which in normal times would be August Bank Holiday. Although work, to-morrow, is to continue as usual, the British determination to celebrate a holiday somehow is obvious to the most casual spectator. Never since last September have I seen the Park so crowded or the orators so numerous. Pushing my way through the massed audiences round the speakers' stands, I recall the words of Douglas

Jerrold: "If an earthquake were to engulf England to-morrow, the English would manage to meet and dine somewhere among the rubbish, just to celebrate the event."

Round Marble Arch, the usual contingent of world-redeemers are proclaiming their creeds. Amongst many platforms which I cannot reach, I notice International Socialism, the Salvation Army, the National Secular Society, the Ministry of Information, the Catholic Evidence Guild, "Reincarnation," and the New and Latter House of Israel. The last is represented by a shabby old man with a workman's cap and a long white beard, to whom no one is listening. A woman in black walks through the crowd, with a poster mysteriously inscribed "The Coming of the Lord" hung round her neck. Passing behind the Ministry of Information, a group of Welsh miners singing hymns in unison temporarily drown the efforts of the speaker to assure his audience that all Empires but the British Empire have been built upon domination.

"Remarkably like a frog he looks!" comments a sceptical woman on the edge of the crowd.

Two adjacent platforms, the Peace Pledge Union and the Anti-Fifth Column League, between them attract the largest circle of perspiring listeners. When a noisy indefatigable heckler seems likely to cause a breach of the peace, the young pacifist wisely abandons his meeting. His hearers drift across to the Anti-Fifth Columnist, whose peculiar brand of vituperative eloquence betrays an obsession with three *bêtes noires*—Mr. Duff Cooper and his new "Silent Column" campaign, Lord Haw-Haw, and the British Union of Fascists.

"I have no political axe to grind," he announces by way of introduction. "We are not the Peace Pledge Union."

"What a pity!" comes a voice from the crowd.

"They're all Jews that speak there," says a girl *sotto voce*, pointing to the Anti-Fifth Columnist's platform. "My Gawd, they've got this country and no mistake!"

"Ever seen such tripe as the Silent Column!" the speaker thunders on. "Walk about with faces like dish-rags, don't say a word! . . . Lord Haw-Haw—yes, that's Bill Joyce—a cowardly rat if ever there was one. . . . Don't you know I'm trying to crush the rottenest filthiest ideology—kill this dirty murderer of children and his rotten gang! . . ."

The crowd listens indulgently. Their several expressions of mild amusement suggest that children slain in Hull or Hamburg are as unreal to them as Alfred Duff Cooper and William Joyce. The sound and fury of the orator's hatred does not in the least represent the feelings of the majority, who regard Hitler as a dangerous but pitiable lunatic, and his bombing pilots as "poor boys" who are lucky to be out of it when they are taken prisoner.

Above the massed untidy heads, the barrage balloons hang low beneath thundrous clouds. Indifferent to the competitive voices of the speakers, a young man in grey flannels and a black Homburg hat is reading "Guilty Men" in its canary-yellow jacket. Round the green Church Army Wilson Carlile Hut for H.M. Forces, soldiers and tired civilians of all ages and both sexes lie stretched asleep on the grass in the hot sunshine.

Some distance from the rostrums, another section of holiday-makers surges incongruously round the fenced-in military area which causes the centre of Hyde Park in this war to resemble the back of the Western Front in the last. I notice several fathers and mothers, their shoes comfortably kicked off, resting their backs against the anti-aeroplane sand-heaps while they eat their sandwiches out of paper bags. Despite repeated exhortations to evacuation, they have brought their families to town for the day. Between the scattered groups, blue-grey pigeons with mauve-tinted breasts strut amiably over the grass, fluttering a little in mild protest when the children chase them. At the bottom of one long diametrical trench, several boys and girls are making pies with the perilous assistance of discarded tins. One charming baby, dressed only in a pair of pink and blue check gingham knickers, plays blithely on the top of a dugout reinforced with piles of sandbags. Only a few yards from the barbed-wire entanglements, a laughing throng drinks its cups of tea beneath the orange umbrellas of the open-air restaurant. On the Serpentine in the distance, hundreds of holiday-makers are boating and bathing from Lansbury's Lido, instituted by the venerable pacifist for the people of London in days before his creed had set him at variance with his party.

At such a time as the present, this characteristic scene could hardly be found in any country but Britain. Remembering my American friends in periods of international crisis, I recall also their habit of excitedly listening by day and night to the radio broadcasts coming through on their perfect transmitters from half the capitals of Europe. The state of tension produced by this keen, nervous, intelligent interest is something, I feel, which an English Bank Holiday crowd would regard with amazement. I recollect that last September, just before he went to the Continent to gather the material for his vivid little study, *Inside Germany,* my friend Oswald Garrison Villard, ex-editor of the American *Nation,* told me that the complete absence of alarm and excitement impressed him more than anything in London.

Though I shudder at the bare possibility of an air-raid in that crowded park with its scores of pretty children, I cannot help wishing that Herr Hitler and Dr. Goebbels could be transported here to inspect the vast London population which they have so often described as panic-stricken. So accustomed has that imperturbable populace now become to military preparations of the most sinister type, that they have ceased to think of their meaning or even to notice them—except as props for their backs or convenient sandpits for their toddlers.

Walking through the Park towards Kensington, with its tall church spire, a monument of serenity, lifted high above the trees beyond the Round Pond, I plunge into speculation about the merits and demerits of our national equanimity. Admirable as it is in one sense, it has disadvantages arising from its close relation to apathy, inertia, lack of foresight and failure of imagination, which is not always fully realised by us who love our country and its people.

That night I listen to Viscount Gort, V.C., broadcasting during the Sunday evening service. Though we have failed, he states, as a nation of worshippers, we are responsible neither for the ambitions of the leaders of the great nations who are to-day our enemies, nor for the failure of their peoples to check their lust for domination. But is it indeed true to say that we have no responsibility for those calamities? Once they were in the saddle, we were not to blame for the rate at which the ambitions of the Nazi leaders grew; but how far was the post-war humiliation of the conquered by the conqueror responsible not only for the driving venomous bitterness of those ambitions, but for the fact that the men who entertain them got into the saddle at all?

For fourteen years after Versailles, there were elements in Germany which feared the rise of Hitlerism and foresaw its consequences more clearly than we did. They knew that Fascism was being created by the policy of the Allies and especially by that of France. The people of this country did nothing to support those German elements or to stop that French policy. They founded their little businesses, bought their little houses on the instalment system, and worked in their little gardens on Saturday afternoons. In their cheerful, contented apathy, they left the circumstances which made Hitler's triumphs inevitable to be created by a group of politicians whom the anonymous "Cato," in the yellow-jacketed book which I have recently seen a young man reading, describes as "Guilty Men."

Even I know from my own limited experience how little interest the liberty-loving democracy of this country took in the actions and policy of France during those vanished days when it was still possible to save the peace of Europe. I remember, throughout 1923, speaking up and down England in protest against France's occupation of the Ruhr. I spoke to tiny audiences, benevolent but a little sceptical of the consequences of French policy as foreseen by a girl in her twenties. But young as I was, I was right in what I foresaw. Any intelligent person who troubled to study the situation could have been as right as I was. But all too few did trouble. The rest were too cheerful, imperturbable, casual, good-humoured and unconcerned. It requires a tense, informed, energetic people, such as the Americans, to perceive long beforehand the Shape of Things to Come.

Over and over again, since this Second Great War of my lifetime began, I have asked myself why the eager, well-meaning peace movement of the 1920's failed so completely to shape the course of international policies. Why I failed. Why Winifred Holtby failed. Why the hard-working men and women who shared our platforms failed in their turn. In Hyde Park, on this twenty-sixth anniversary of the outbreak of the First World War, I have found one answer to the question which I asked myself in a New Forest cottage on September 3, 1939. This answer comes from those selfsame qualities which make us both a great, much-enduring people in adversity, and a set of complacent ostriches in prosperity.

We failed because we were too easily satisfied. We assumed that the keen enthusiasm of an energetic minority signified a desire for peace on the part of the whole nation. Perhaps it did; but it signified only a negative, apathetic desire which was never sufficiently alive to count the cost of peace and be ready to pay it. I remember the excitement of the League of Nations Union—a real influence for peace during those early years in which we who were young believed ourselves to be building a new heaven and a new earth—when its membership touched a quarter of a million. It should not have been excited. It should have been beating its metaphorical breast because a quarter of a million is only one two-hundredth part of a population of fifty millions. For again and again, when those crises occurred in which a different decision might have led Europe away from instead of towards the precipice, it was not the quarter-million, but the forty-nine and three-quarter millions, who decided (or rather, failed to reverse) the policy of this country.

We are an admirable, imperturbable, good-tempered, kindly people. With pride I assert that our equable endurance through months of deepening nightmare will remain a national saga so long as history is written and read. Yet I hope that, when the occasion for a peace settlement comes once more, we shall not again accept cheerfulness, patience, composure and good-natured resignation as desirable substitutes for energy, knowledge, foresight, vitality and intelligence. We need both varieties of national quality if we are to build, this time, a structure that will endure.

12. "FIFTEEN SEASICK CHILDREN"

AT THE OFFICES of the Children's Overseas Reception Board in Berkeley Street off Piccadilly, we are working overtime interviewing escorts.

Already 200,000 children are registered for emigration to the Dominions, and our next task is to make a list of dependable travellers ready to accompany them. One of the escorts chosen is named Mary Cornish; she is a music teacher from Baker Street. She impresses us as courageous and responsible, but we shall not know the full measure of her quality until late in September, after she has kept six boys alive for eight days in a lifeboat from the torpedoed *City of Benares.*

Since Richard and Hilary sailed from Liverpool, I have been working in this new and hastily constituted government department, with its five hundred members recruited from less harassed branches of the Civil Service. The news of the children's safe arrival in Montreal, awaited through hours of nightmare-ridden darkness, has sent me in gratitude to Fate and the Americans to do what I can to hasten the departure of others.

"The train journey to St. Paul only took two days," writes Hilary from Minnesota. "In the train all the people were awfully friendly and gave us meals and iced drinks, and sweets at their own expense. Indeed they kept coming one after another and didn't stop until the train did."

"You know, Mummie," confides Richard in a later letter, "I never thought we could have such lovely times in America."

In Berkeley Street, the upper floors of Messrs. Thomas Cook & Son's huge building have been taken over for the work of C.O.R.B. At first, through the brazen days of London's hottest August, we interview the would-be escorts in pairs on the edge of a long table, with groups of three chairs arranged round it, in an airless first-floor room which looks into a well. But now we have moved up another floor into a large office which gives each couple of interviewers a desk and two chairs that at least endow us with a semblance of dignity.

Half a mile away in Park Lane, the American Committee for the overseas evacuation of British children is working on its own scheme in the ballroom of Grosvenor House. I call there one day on official business, and observe the gold chairs, the thick pile carpets, and the subdued lights so strangely favoured by Americans even when they are typewriting or reading manuscript letters. Everything I see—the tinted globes which shade the lights, the large desks with beautiful clean blotting paper, the neat typed cards for escorts with their photographs attached—reaches the highest possible standard of elegant efficiency.

Mentally I compare our casual British office. How, I wonder, would the well-groomed young women working at Grosvenor House appreciate our hard tin chairs and undusted room, where the black soot on the top of the wall cupboards lies too thick for our hats and coats to be laid there? What would they think of our rough notes about the personalities of escorts, made, not on fine quality cards with large luxurious typewriters, but on sheets torn off halfpenny pads and inscribed with hard Government pencils? Our office, like most English offices, is a combination of a public lavatory and a railway station waiting room, but the escorts who apply to us or the Americans, and sometimes to both, are very much the same. Good, bad and indifferent (by far the greatest number being in the last of these three categories), they appear in their dozens day by day, and apply for a job of whose nature some have only the vaguest understanding.

My fellow interviewer, an experienced member of a religious emigration society, gives stability to my writer's habit of studying the psychology of my fellow men and women. In collaboration we put to the applicants a succession of standard questions.

"What experience have you of looking after children in groups?"

"Oh, plenty!" the average applicant cheerfully replies. "I used to put my sister's three boys to bed when I stayed at their farm."

"But have you ever taken charge of Girl Guides—or done camping, or settlement work, or taken Sunday school outings, or helped at child welfare centres?"

"Oh—er—no. Nothing *public* like that."

We pass on to the next series of necessary qualifications.

"And how much sea-travelling have you done?"

"Oh, any amount! We've been to the Continent for our holiday every year for the past ten years. And then my parents live in the Isle of Wight."

"But haven't you sailed anything more exacting than the Channel? Have you crossed the Atlantic, or been to India or South Africa?"

"Oh—er—no. Nothing like *that*. But then my husband

always says that if you can cross the Channel without being seasick, you can really go anywhere."

At this stage we take the initiative.

"Do you realise precisely what this job of being an escort will mean?"

"Well—not exactly. I imagined you'd tell me."

"What you will have to do is to take charge of fifteen children, probably of all ages and both sexes, and look after them on the boat from start to finish. You'll have to assume as much responsibility as if you were their mother, wherever you go and whatever the conditions. It will mean getting them up, putting them to bed, seeing that they go to their meals and eat the proper food, as well as keeping them amused all through the voyage. If you're chosen for Africa or Australia, it will involve going blacked-out through the tropics—which must be pretty stuffy, I imagine, though I haven't tried it. And if it's the Atlantic it's certain to be rough, and you may find yourself in charge of fifteen seasick children all the way across. So, you see, it isn't exactly a picnic."

"No-o. It does sound a pretty hard job."

"It is. We have to put it to you at its worst, you see, because it's no good people applying who imagine that they're going to get a pleasant sea voyage for the benefit of their health. And then there's no actual salary. It isn't a way of making money; it's a form of service."

"Well, I did know that. I don't want any pay. But that paper I got said something about allowances."

"Yes. You get a small bonus for each voyage so that you're not out of pocket. It's £5 for Canada, £12 for South Africa and £20 for Australia. But then if you go to Australia under present conditions, you might easily be away for four or five months."

As the would-be escort gets up to depart, shaken but not yet wholly deterred from an adventure which appears less roseate than it did, I put one final question.

"Can you swim?"

The applicant looks startled and unhappy.

"Well—yes. I can swim the length of the Baths, and a bit more in the sea. But I can't life-save or anything like that. The instructions didn't say it was necessary."

"We hope it won't be, but you may well find it a useful qualification. Even with all the care that can be taken, you can't rule out the chance of an emergency nowadays."

I speak more prophetically than I know, for although thousands of children will be conveyed through "seavacuation" to safety, tragedy is to be written into the history of C.O.R.B. At the end of August, a liner carrying 320 British children to Canada will be torpedoed without the loss of a single life, but late in September more than seventy children—as dear to their parents as Richard and Hilary are to us—will vanish, pitiful victims of war, into the cold raging waves of the North Atlantic when their storm-battered ship is struck by torpedo or mine. Five out of the nine escorts will go to their deaths in a noble but fruitless endeavour to save the lives of the children in their care. More than a week after the wreck, six little boys and their escorts, Mary Cornish and Father O'Sullivan, will come literally back from the dead when a Sunderland flier discovers a lifeboat with forty-six survivors which has been afloat for eight days in huge hostile seas.

At the end of each hot London day, we usually find that our cross-examination has eliminated the less promising applicants. These include persons of all types who hope that by acting as escorts they can escape from the impending bombs to Canada, South Africa or Australia—a possibility now open under wartime regulations only to returning Colonials, men and women whose normal business takes them overseas, wives joining their husbands abroad, girls crossing the ocean to get married, children under sixteen or veterans over sixty, and persons undertaking work regarded as important by erratic government departments.

The "escapists" are seldom so numerous as the middle-aged women without special qualifications who are looking for a job or even more vaguely for "war work." Never before have I realised how universal to-day are the tragedies of unoccupied spinsterhood, stranded widowhood, or the lonely wifehood of women whose children have grown up and whose husbands are serving in Army, Navy or Air Force. Sometimes, by way of variety, it is the men who are stranded; through our offices stream a long procession of unemployed actors, couriers, entertainers and cinema managers whose genial peacetime occupation has completely disappeared. Before we have interviewed applicants for a week, we could make a long list of the civilised forms of employment connected with amusement, travel, music, art and the stage, which have been slaughtered by the grim inexorability of war.

It is a relief to turn from these blameless but unsuitable victims of catastrophe to the escorts whom we can gladly employ—the welfare workers and Guide leaders, the more human types of teacher, the extra-intelligent nursery nurses, the chaplains, headmasters, Scout officers and retired energetic officials. We count it a red-letter day when we interview the ex-police administrator from India and his tough, humane wife; another when we discover the headmistress of an elementary school who leaves us with the confident impression that she could run the Navy.

At the end of two or three weeks, after interviewing an average of thirty men and women a day, we discuss those whom we especially remember for some dramatic circumstance or outstanding eccentricity; they form a fair sample of our daily applicants.

"What were the Christian names of that woman who said she was a Seventh Day Adventist?"

"Theosebia Ernestina. It was the Spiritualist who called herself Ruby Esmeralda."

"That wasn't the one who said she was born in 1987?"

"Oh, no! It was she who told us that her husband was partner of Malcolm MacDonald who built the Victoria Falls and is now Ministry of Health. You remember—she said she'd never trained for anything because she was a rich girl who lived in Grosvenor Street."

Mutually we picture some of the others—the theatrical manager aged seventy-four who had taken parties of young actresses to Canada; the fair-haired eighteen-year-old child who came to us with reddened eyelids because she had learnt only the previous evening that her fiancé had died as a prisoner of war; the Canadian clergyman with a strong sense of melodrama whose ship had been torpedoed on the voyage to England; the dictatorial Mayfair matron who had shepherded refugees from Paris and expected to get a job as escort by bullying her interviewers; the young Rhodes scholar with black eyebrows and blue-grey eyes who was returning to New Zealand to join the Army; the muscular and intimidating circus phenomenon who could remain under water for over an hour and confidently introduced himself as "Attila, the Human Fish."

Walking towards Hyde Park Corner as the August evening cools to sunset, my fellow interviewer and I discuss these and many others. There is one test, I tell him, which I apply to all the escorts: "Are you a person whom I would have put in charge of Richard and Hilary when they went to America?"

The loss of the French fleet, as we now know, has reduced the large, imaginative scheme conceived by Geoffrey Shakespeare for child emigration to a small experimental plan; not one hundred thousand children, but perhaps no more than ten thousand will this year be able to start their lives again with a reassuring ocean between themselves and the suicidal quarrels of the exhausted Old World. But our work as interviewers will not be wasted, for no one knows how long the scheme will continue, or how many escorts may be required in the end.

Already, to find five hundred dependable men and women, the members of the Advisory Panel have between them interviewed fifteen thousand. At night their faces, their clothes, their answers to my questions, come constantly into my dreams, and I awaken to hear myself repeating the standard question: "And could you take the full responsibility for fifteen seasick children? . . ."

13. ONCE RESIDENTIAL

OF THE FIVE LARGE HOUSES at the eastern end of the terrace, our own is still the only one occupied. Everywhere "To LET" notices decorate front gates and balconies; the back gardens are desolations of weeds and long grass. In the ribbon of riverside park which runs along the Embankment the carefully tended flowers still bloom, but each section now contains an air-raid shelter thickly covered with earth where plantains and dandelions are sprouting.

A row of little luxury houses, built just before the war in a street connecting the Embankment with the King's Road, Chelsea, wears the half-surprised, forlorn air of habitations which have never been used. Through dirty windows the passer-by looks into empty rooms; the tiny paved gardens are choked with sorrel. At the entrance of a passageway leading to a well-equipped modern welfare centre which is now used as an auxiliary fire station, a notice board still stands inscribed: "Danger! Children!" The danger is certainly there, in forms not contemplated by the sign-writer, but the children have gone.

In Chelsea's pleasant squares, the spaces where garden chairs once stood and fairy cycles dashed to and fro, are now taken over by A.R.P. squadrons or barrage balloon units. To my generation, each public square so used brings back memories of the area just behind the lines in the last war. The inhabitants of the surrounding houses have found either these memories too poignant, or the threat of the raids which are already battering England too intimidating. More houses are offered for sale each week; the August sunlight shines from the perpetually cloudless sky on to the dusty floors of empty basement kitchens. Even in those homes which are only temporarily abandoned, the pictures have been removed and laid face downwards, the glass packed away in tissue-paper or sawdust; the family silver deposited in the bank. With good reason, as experience has already shown, the absent householders fear the depredations of looters who may enter through shattered windows almost as much as they dread the havoc of raids.

It is August 14th, the day before the date allotted by Hitler for his triumphal entry into London. All round the coast from the chalk cliffs of Dover to the iron cranes of Southampton, his aeroplanes are bombing up the Channel. In New York, we learn, crowds are scanning throughout the night the flaming headlines in special editions of the newspapers. Yet except for her balloons and sandbags London, the ultimate objective of these mass attacks, looks much the same as usual. There are no excited preparations for Hitler's proposed arrival. The Band of the Coldstream Guards is playing Gilbert and Sullivan on the roof of an air-raid shelter in Trafalgar Square; sales are busily in progress in the Oxford Street stores; the Union Jack flying from Buckingham Palace proclaims that the King has not departed to Canada.

The newsvendors, in particular, appear to have no ominous apprehensions about the morrow. Now that the paper shortage has put an end to posters, they make their own announcements in white chalk on large brown placards. As I walk down Piccadilly, I stop to read some of the more conspicuous:

BIGGEST RAID EVER. SCORE 78 TO 26. ENGLAND STILL BATTING.

YES, BILL. NAZI PLANES ARE MADE IN GERMANY AND FINISHED IN ENGLAND.

HITLER POPPIN' THEM UP AND OUR TEAM STILL POPPIN' 'EM DOWN.

At Hyde Park Corner a pavement artist has reproduced Guido Reni's National Gallery portrait of the suffering Christ, "*Ecce Homo.*" Below his rendering of the tortured bleeding face, he has chalked Burns' lines:

> Man's inhumanity to man
> Makes countless thousands mourn.

To-day I have an afternoon of freedom from the office, and for once can have tea beside the open French window of my pleasant Chelsea drawing-room overlooking the Thames. Nearly a quarter of a century ago, I went forth as a young girl to seek the war in the Archipelago, in the Mediterranean, in France. To-day I have no need to seek it, for it has come to me. Sitting in front of my window, I can watch it go by without stirring a yard.

Right opposite our house are a variety of defence preparations which will fulfil their purpose in the event of an invasion. Along the Embankment, between the bridge and my window, the war passes in the shape of innumerable vehicles: camouflaged cars and lorries carrying guns beneath painted tarpaulins; A.R.P ambulances; dispatch riders on motor cycles going at sixty miles an hour; waggons carrying loads of waste paper and other forms of salvage. Incongruously mingled with these military conveyances comes the civilian traffic: small cars belonging to suburban dwellers going home from their work; scarlet omnibuses run by London Transport; vans belonging to Lyons' Ice Cream and the London Steam Carpet Co.; men and women cyclists and pedestrians. Many of the women, even in the centre of London, have now given up the habit of wearing hats.

Up and down the shining river pass grey-painted tugs which resemble small war craft, and little L.D.V. launches used by the river units of the Home Guards. A large yacht converted into an ambulance boat is moored to a quay fifty yards from our door. In the Embankment Gardens, a steel-helmeted air-raid warden inspects the new underground shelters.

By sitting in my own window for half an hour, I can see as much war preparation as I saw in Étaples village during 1917. In those days, the London newspapers used to remark that the Zeppelin raids "brought it home to us." It is coming home to us now in deed and in truth.

We in London have not much longer to wait.

14. MAIN-LINE TERMINUS

AUGUST 15TH IS HERE AT LAST, but Hitler and Mussolini have still failed to arrive. Instead, by their surprise afternoon raid on Croydon, they will cause the first London siren for two months to usher in the three weeks of pre-Blitzkrieg which will warn the capital of what is to come.

As I walk over Westminster Bridge to the main-line terminus, London wears, as always, the calm appearance of an old engraving delicately outlined against a tranquil sky. But the wooden barricades against the parapets and the barbed-wire entanglements round the County Hall remind me that she cannot hope to retain undamaged much longer the serene Victorian contours which represent, for my generation, the city that we know.

Across the Bridge and beyond the terminus stretches the sprawling bulk of the suburbs and their population— like ants crawling over the biggest bombing target on the face of this earth. But though the station is a major military objective and a nerve-centre of England's transport, its numerous platforms, on this warm afternoon of late summer, maintain a peaceful, somnolent air. Little dusty trains run placidly past their signals from the bombarded South Coast. A large part of the glass roof is now covered with tarpaulin, but enough glass remains to cause many casualties if the raiders come. Through the crevices of the tarpaulin, the August sunshine glints downwards into the grimy restaurant windows. Although wooden barricades protect the entrances to offices and waiting rooms, the day seems created for seaside holidays, and the terminus a gateway to life rather than death.

Yet, for so many men and women of England, it is death and not life to which the coast-bound coaches carry them. On a loaded trolley comes a group of blue-jackets bound for some nameless vessel, their canvas knapsacks over their shoulders and their kit-bags piled in front of their feet. A platoon of Home Guards, many of them wearing 1914–1918 ribbons on their stiff new khaki, marches smartly past the platform barrier. Below the "Departures" indicator, soldiers of the Regular Army, their steel helmets strapped to their backs, stand drinking tea round a trolley containing chocolates, cigarettes, a pile of sad-looking pasties, and a collection of cardboard cartons labelled "Snack Lunch Box, 1/–."

A few weeks ago, a friend of mine was here when he observed a dozen German prisoners being marshalled across the station by five military policemen. The prisoners were halted just as a train arrived packed with tired British soldiers in soiled battle dress. As they alighted, a burst of cheering came from the crowd of waiting passengers; the soldiers were a detachment of survivors brought across the Channel from Dunkirk by the "Saucy Sallies." The German prisoners, my friend noticed, cheered as loudly as the rest. When the men from Dunkirk marched past them, the Germans turned up their thumbs. . . .

Outside Platform 7, I observe a notice board which stoutly maintains the British reputation for understatement:

Southern Railway

NOTICE

In consequence of the line being obstructed by

MISHAP

Passengers are warned that trains proceeding To (or From)
X., Y., and Z
will be delayed

By Order.

All over the station there are other notices to remind the intending traveller that England is at war.

"Under directions given by the Regional Commissioners under Defence (General) Regulation 16a," reads one, "persons are prohibited from entering for the purpose of a holiday, recreation or pleasure, areas served by the following stations."

The names of 705 stations follow. They range from Berwick-on-Tweed, round the East and South coasts, to Weymouth and Portland; soon they will be continued to Land's End.

Beside the main entrance, a news theatre advertises two outstanding titles in its list of attractions: "Air Battle over the South-East Coast" and "Fools Who Made History." Close by, a small yellow placard with a pointing arrow indicates the way to the first-aid post. Travellers who include the usual heterogeneous gathering of girls in summer frocks, shabbily dressed young men with suitcases, and stout women carrying babies, are warned by another large printed announcement that they use the station air-raid shelter "entirely AT THEIR OWN RISK." On the bookstall of W. H. Smith & Son, the titles most prominently displayed are "Ships of the Royal Navy," "Aircraft of the British Empire," and Louis Bromfield's "Night in Bombay." A red Royal Mail van, driving into the yard from the outside world, carries a pious injunction supplied by the Ministry of Information:

CARELESS TALK COSTS LIVES. IF YOU MUST TALK, TALK VICTORY.

I watch the trains imperturbably leaving for one of the areas where a "mishap" has occurred. Before and after they reach the repaired bomb crater, they will pass through stations without names, and run across open country where roads are unmarked and bewildered motorists will desperately endeavour to obtain directions from wary farmers who have been explicitly warned against parachutists and Fifth Columnists. The county surveyors' stores are piled with crossbars that once guided wayfarers to Smugglers' Bay or Marshington-on-Moor; the mass obliteration of local signs has imposed a new form of democracy on hotels which can no longer advertise themselves as "Oldhaven's Best" or "The First in Seaport."

Yet the task of defeating parachutists is still incomplete, for local stationers continue to display picture postcards on outside stalls, and road maps giving details of each district can be picked up for two or three shillings. There is even a projected onslaught on tombstones, which so often mention the locality of the commemorated dead. Those who have never started on the job could hardly conceive the difficulties of imposing anonymity even upon a village.

The trains running from the main-line terminus are not

yet impeded by sirens, but a few weeks later the number of London "alerts" will have amounted to hundreds. At first the booking offices will close during raids, but later their work will continue uninterrupted. The trains themselves will leave on time after a loud speaker has informed the travellers: "An air-raid warning has just been sounded. Passengers can go to the shelters or proceed by their trains."

I cannot recall seeing a single passenger go to a shelter after finding a seat in a coach where there is at least protection against falling shrapnel and glass splinters from the platform roof. Even when guns are firing and fighting aeroplanes zooming above the station, the whistle will blow, the guard wave his flag, and the 5.20 for Somewhere on the South Coast proceed on its way. Until the train reaches the limit of the air-raid zone, it will keep to a maximum speed of fifteen miles an hour. On entering the all-clear zone, it will be stopped at the first signal cabin, where the driver will learn that the all-clear has gone. Then the train will continue at its normal speed, eventually arriving late but triumphant at its destination.

Even the tearing up of rails and the bombing of bridges will cause the station to close only for a few days. Like England, like London, like her raided population, the main-line terminus must carry on.

15. THE RAIDERS COME TO TOWN

FOR THE FIRST TIME, on an August afternoon, the Nazi
raiders penetrate within the London area, and drop their
bombs upon an astonished residential district in the
South-West.

Twice in the day, the sirens go. They have now sounded
three times within twenty-four hours—a new and alarming
experience for London.

When the midday siren goes I am sitting in our back
garden in the sunshine, writing an article in defence of
our traditional liberties for a little newspaper read by men
and women who for years have used their energies in an
attempt to prevent war. Some day peace will return,
though many of this country's citizens will not live to see
it, and a few of us believe that, in preparation for the
distant hour, we must endeavour to keep alive the peacetime values of charity, truth, and compassion. Not least we
must preserve with determination those minority rights
which are an essential part of the liberties that our young
pilots are ready to defend with their lives.

"You'd better come in!" calls Martin from the study
window. Reluctantly I pick up my papers and go, for the
August sunshine is pleasant, and I have only been in the
garden for half an hour.

Through the open French windows of the drawing-room come distant explosive sounds which might equally well be gunfire or traffic along Chelsea Embankment. The rest of the household has already assembled in the front half of the coal cellar which has become our air-raid shelter. Is it necessary to join them, we wonder. Work is urgent, and there is no sound of aeroplanes overhead. We pull the sofa away from the window and, sitting down side by side, continue to write. Shall I be able, I wonder, to finish my article, knowing that bombs may drop at any moment? Or shall I share the disabilities of my young temporary cook, who finds it "so difficult to concentrate" on lunch or dinner when the sirens go?

Looking up, I see the few passers-by quietly walking into the air-raid shelter beneath the Embankment Gardens. The buses, in accordance with their usual practice of stopping for passengers who wish to take cover and then continuing their journey, go quietly on their way only half empty. A few cars speed along the Embankment without a pause. The men working on the pontoon bridge opposite our house lay down their tools and prepare to run across the road to the shelter, but until bombs begin to fall they prefer resting in their conspicuous position in the sunshine to waiting in the underground darkness.

Although, subconsciously, I am watching and listening, my mind unexpectedly continues to function. In one hour the little article for peace-lovers is completed, incongruously written in the midst of war. We look at the hot empty street and wonder. There is no movement and no more noise. What is happening in some other part of London? Who is damaged, suffering, dying? Suddenly, then, the all-clear goes. The passers-by emerge from their shelter, and life along the Embankment continues as before.

Later, the same afternoon, the sirens sound again. This time, I am engaged in my usual work of interviewing escorts at the Children's Overseas Reception Board. The last few applicants have just arrived for their appointments, when the air-raid warden's whistle summons us to the huge underground shelters in the basement of Cook's Building. As the sirens wail, the interviewers—some philosophically grumbling because their interviews were not quite finished and they will be obliged to come back to them—troop down three flights of stone steps in company with five hundred men and girl clerks.

Downstairs we gather into the six or seven connecting basement shelters. Only a few seats have been provided, so most of the five hundred are obliged to stand. At first the girls and men laugh and chatter. A very few, more apprehensive than the rest, lean back with closed eyes against the wall. Some who are lucky enough to possess them read newspapers. A colleague offers me half her chair, and I begin to write the reports of my two previous interviews.

For all that any of us know in the crowded basement, the streets of London may be burning above our heads. We hear constant crashes; they may come from the traffic above, the Underground Railway below, or from Nazi bombs. We wonder again who is "going through it"—and where. A sentence from the last war comes back into my head; it was written to me twenty-five years ago by an ex-schoolboy in Flanders listening to the bombardment of Ypres: "Somebody's getting hell, but it isn't you—yet."

Later we shall learn that, as we sat there, the first bombers to pass London's defences have destroyed a church, a club, a District Railway station, and several rows of suburban houses. New York, excitedly listening-in at midday to the London broadcast, hears the sound of the warning sirens and the crash of guns.

In the shelter, a few of the girls hide their faces as they wait. They are not afraid; they are probably thinking of young men, whose lives were before them, falling from the sky and crashing in flames on the ground. The young men of both sides. Those orators and broadcasters who treat war as though it were a blood-sport and describe it in terms of a cup-tie final, do not represent the spirit of ordinary British men and women who offer cups of tea to crashed German pilots, or go out to rescue them in small boats when they fall into the Channel.

We stay below the ground for over an hour. The air-conditioning plant which is supposed to operate has failed. At the end of half the period, the danger of asphyxiation appears at least as great as the risk of damage by bombs. Silence gradually descends upon the waiting crowd of workers. Fortunately my reports are finished, for the heavy atmosphere has completely obliterated my powers of concentration. Dimly I begin to understand the preliminary sufferings of sailors, English or German, who dive to their death in submarines. The air-raid wardens and their Red Cross assistants walk round the basement squirting disinfectant into the air. Just as some of the frailer inhabitants of the shelters begin to look like requiring their assistance, a shrill whistle blows through the building.

"It's the all-clear at last! Come on! Come on!"

The young girl clerks scamper up the stairway. Their elders, with throbbing temples, follow more slowly. I stand, half suffocated, in the open doorway. Outside, in the glittering unchanged expanse of Piccadilly, the traffic is again on the move. I go upstairs and interview the capable young applicant who has patiently waited for an hour in the shelter. Since we both have excruciating headaches the interview proceeds slowly and without animation, but she gets enough of her personality across to justify a recommendation.

In Piccadilly, the soft air of the summer evening seems gentler and more benevolent than usual. Pedestrians, pale but animated, are speculating about the locality of the raid. How many will go home to find their houses damaged, their relatives killed or injured? What has happened, I ask myself, to Martin on his way to his week-end settlement work in Bermondsey? In spite of my anxiety for him, my headache vanishes as I walk quickly through Knightsbridge and Sloane Street to Chelsea.

At home everything is normal, and I learn that Martin, after spending the raid period in a Charing Cross restaurant, has telephoned reporting his own safety and inquiring after mine.

16. SUBURBAN AFTERMATH

DURING THE WEEK which follows my afternoon in the air-raid shelter, an ambulance driver from the raided district invites me to see the damage. Over luncheon she tells me how the local population have reacted to the raid.

"It's queer," she says, "how differently people I've known all my life have taken it. Half an hour after it was over, some of them were out shopping as though nothing had happened. Others have been so apprehensive ever since, that the moment the siren goes they rush for shelter."

"Did you find your A.R.P. services worked all right?" I ask her.

"They stood the strain, but only just. You see, we never expected a raid of that size in a residential area. To me, it seemed just like one of the many practices we've had; I couldn't get into my head, somehow, that this time it was real . . . The reaction came the next day, when I felt too tired to move."

"How much of it did you remember afterwards—or was it all just confused?"

"It was mostly like a sort of vague nightmare. The only thing I remember clearly was somebody saying to me: 'Can you get an ambulance quickly to High Path?' . . . And

I couldn't—there was no one to send. We all had too much to do as it was."

After luncheon, she drives me out to a district where the first signs of damage are a number of blown-in windows along a main road. Except for this fringe of little camouflaged buildings, the area has no military objective. A mile or two farther on, we come to a crossroads where a bomb has fallen on the central roundabout. The roads surrounding this huge crater are oddly undamaged, and the traffic is proceeding at its normal pace. But the small hotel at the corner—a pleasure place with an outdoor restaurant and coloured umbrellas—has a startled, shattered appearance, like a drunken man who has wakened in the morning to wonder where he spent the night. Its windows are blown in and their frames are askew; the striped awnings are torn and the chimneys have fallen. The bushes in the garden look dishevelled, as though an army has been fighting amongst them.

Two or three hundred yards further down the wide suburban road, we come to several railed-off streets. Here a number of small houses have been completely demolished; their neighbours all have damaged roofs and boarded-up windows. This, the ambulance driver tells me, is an area of "small people"; its dainty, jerry-built villas have been bought on the instalment plan by bank-clerks and business managers. Here is all the pathos of war; we contemplate the incongruity of this gentle, placid existence with the overwhelming tragedy brought by modern international quarrels upon the innocent and the unsophisticated. These neat little homes were never planned to withstand the metalled might of Nazi Germany.

As we drive back towards the main shopping district, we pass two funerals. Though the victims have evidently been poor, their coffins are lavishly covered with flowers. The "negligible casualties" so often reported in the Press are not negligible to the pale men and women in black whose car follows the hearse.

"They've been going on all the week," tersely comments my companion.

We pass a corner whence one or two of the dead must surely have come. Here a garage has been reduced to four blackened walls surrounding heaps of glass and unidentifiable debris. Against the first-floor wall of a room that must once have been a kitchen, a black cooking-stove hangs in mid-air. Like all disorder, the wrecked garage possesses a sordidness beyond description. Close beside it, a large men's club and a public house have also been damaged. Outside a stationer's shop stands a chalked exhortation: "Boys of the R.A.F. Bomber Squadron— Remember our area when you are next over Germany." At conspicuous corners all over the borough, various notices invite contributions to the "Local Distress Fund."

The District Railway station has been partly demolished; it is now operating with determined regularity behind boarded-up offices and matchboard partitions. Not far away is High Path, whence the call for an ambulance came. The need must have been urgent, for here is a mutilated row of pleasant semi-business dwelling houses occupied by jobbing builders and other individual tradesmen. One comfortable-looking residence—three stories of red creeper-covered brick typically known as "Ivydene"— has its side blown away, leaving the sinister impression of a gaping wound in a human flank. The garden gate, of ornamental wood, is broken and riddled; the damaged creeper hangs like torn fabric from the ruined walls. Its neighbour, "Moorfield," also partly destroyed, bears the marks of machine-gun bullets on walls and palings. In a local fair-ground round the corner, several wrecked motor-trailers are standing. The house next door has nothing left but its front façade, where a little Union Jack still flutters forlornly from a broken window.

"The marvellous thing is the way the church escaped," says the ambulance driver, pointing to the large building standing erect amid the devastation, untouched except for bullet holes through tower and windows. In the church-yard we find a small stone monument to Lord Nelson, who lived in this district with Lady Hamilton. The little memorial is riddled with bullets; one has obliterated part of the inscription. Two tiny ornamental cannon on either side of the stone provide, by contrast, evidence of the "progress" which a century and a half has brought to the conduct of war. Behind the strangely immune church, a school has suffered; its windows are gone and the frames grotesquely twisted. A large placard outside the door states: "School Closed. Names for Evacuation taken here."

In a working-class street some distance away, war's piti-fulness again appears without its intermittent glamour. Two long rows of small two-storey houses face one another in dreary desolation, doorless and windowless; they are hardly more than skeletons of houses which appear ready to collapse at any moment. Yet many are still inhabited; women in soiled overalls with arms akimbo lean over the damaged window-sills conversing with their neighbours. The house on which the bomb fell has vanished into a heap of rubble, but the walls on either side, though stark and bare, stand up as cleanly as if some titanic axe had sliced them from their neighbour. In the midst of stones and brickdust, carefully cultivated asters and geraniums still bloom bravely, their brightness unimpaired.

At the end of the street is a small greengrocer's shop which has completely escaped injury. The young owner, my guide tells me, was outside the stall polishing his apples a few moments after the raid.

"Where were you at the time?" I inquire.

"I was here," he tells me. "But I got into the cellar pretty quick. Odd thing, the house that got the bomb was empty. The people were away. Only one empty in the row."

Much of the damage in this area, I learn, has been due to delayed-action bombs. Yet in spite of the architectural wounds where ruin and squalor have replaced tranquillity and order, the evidences of Wimbledon's ordeal have to be sought; little would be visible to a passing car, and much less to an aeroplane. It is outside the Town Hall that we find the real record of local tragedy. Here the casualty list informs us that on the day of the Malden and Wimbledon raid—the toll taken by the Nazi raiders in the metropolitan area was 78 killed and 108 injured.

"But you always believe," says the ambulance driver, "that whoever gets it next, it won't be you. That's what enables people to carry on."

17. WARDEN'S POST

THE AIR-RAID WARDEN from Yorkshire and I set out from her flat at midnight to the post in West Kensington.

It is a late summer night of incomparable beauty, with no cloud, no vaporous mist, no breath of wind. On this last day of the old moon, the vault of sky above London is jet-black, with a myriad stars shining down as clearly as though the great threatened city were a serene country village. For the first time for many nights, no heavy hesitant sound of cruising German bombers echoes from the gigantic heavens. Scanning them with tired experienced eyes, we see only the faint intermittent "feeler" of a searchlight, the lightninglike flicker from the Underground Railway, the occasional flash of a shooting star. After two sirens during the day, the usual evening warning has not summoned us to the shelters.

As we walk on through the dark streets, the only audible sounds are the wailing of cats, a whistle from a train, the blast of a ship's hooter from the Thames two miles away. The post, like most wardens' posts in the metropolitan area, has been set up in a London County Council school. The other wardens on duty—a dental mechanic, a shopkeeper, and a paperhanger respectively—sit in a small office with a lofty ceiling. Three *Daily Telegraph* war maps hang from the yellow distempered walls. In a corner the post's mascot—a thin and very lively black cat which walked in as a stray kitten six months ago—consumes his pungent evening meal of milk and fish. The Blue Cross label of the National Society for the Prevention of Cruelty to Animals, hung round his neck, entitles him to preferential treatment in a raid.

Pinned on the notice board are a medley of papers—lists of the wardens' duties and war stations, notices of lectures, a letter of appreciation from the Mayor and Chief Warden of Fulham expressing his satisfaction with the local civil defence work "during the recent public air-raid warnings." The latest list of air-raid casualties in the Metropolitan Police District shows that, between Wednesday August 28th and Thursday August 29th, fifteen civilians were killed and nineteen injured.

We go out again into the area on a patrol of the public shelters. The chief post warden accompanies us, wheeling his bicycle; in peacetime he is a glazier by profession; and he was severely wounded in the War of 1914. Like his colleagues he wears an informal navy blue uniform, resembling a workman's dungarees. When the sirens go he mounts his bicycle and rides round the district, opening the locked shelters, and unlocking the first-aid apparatus and the shovels for dealing with incendiary bombs. If it is not locked up, this equipment provided by the locality for the public benefit is invariably stolen. The thieves are as difficult to detect as the slatterns who leave the shelters littered with newspapers or the greasy wrappings of their fish-and-chips.

These surface shelters, built of brick and roofed with concrete, are reported to withstand any catastrophe but a direct hit from a bomb. They are said to be impervious to bullets and splinters, and the blast from an explosion may rock but will not shatter them. Each thick squat building has an alternative exit filled in with sheet iron or loose bricks which can easily be removed. A dim electric bulb provides illumination. If the raid destroys the local supply of electricity, a lamp padlocked to the ceiling will provide light from its separate battery. Before the London raids have become severe, these shelters are popular owing to the soundproof material which shuts out the noise of anti-aircraft barrage and distant bombs. Later, when several direct hits have shown that they may become death-traps which increase the number of casualties, a widespread agitation for deep shelters will arise, and London's poorer population will invade the Tubes.

Most of the surface shelters are built, or adapted, as annexes to public buildings; one adjoins a church and another a convent; a third is a public laundry reinforced with iron and concrete. The district is humble, with a mainly working-class population inhabiting small two-storey houses without basements or garden shelters. It is for householders who possess neither Anderson steel shelters nor basements, that communal brick buildings are now provided. Even when empty, their limited ventilation and their combined smell of concrete, new brick, and Jeyes' Fluid makes them stuffy and close. When the public are in occupation, the atmosphere almost solidifies.

So far the residents of the small houses have taken to the shelters like foxes to their lairs. They have adopted them so effectively that they now camp there regularly with their blankets and pillows, rather than get up from a warm bed and emerge into the night when the siren goes.

"There's a whole set of social distinctions grown up in these shelters," my friend the warden tells me. "The mutual exclusiveness of members at Yorkshire luncheon clubs is nothing to this. One group will refuse to enter the same shelter as another from their street. Then there are the quiet ones who won't share the shelter with children, and the bright young things who play cards or darts and don't want elderly people. One old man regards a small communal shelter as his personal property; he sits there in his armchair and refuses to let anyone else come in."

"And what about the laundry?" I inquire. "Surely that's too big for these class distinctions?"

"Not at all. A party from the end of the street has adopted it and won't let in strangers if they can help it. They're probably there now. We'll go and see."

We creep into the ex-laundry and find its habitual occupants stretched along the narrow wooden benches. One young man—who is "nervous," I am told, with an amusement which suggests that so far this human quality is rare—lies on his back with his head against the wall and his knees bent upwards. Under him is a folded rug, and over him a white tasselled counterpane which gives him the strange appearance of lying in a shroud. Along another bench a stout, heavy man is stretched fast asleep and snoring loudly. Beside him on a table stands a large bottle of beer and a dirty glass. Not far away, an elderly charwoman in a raincoat and a man's cap rests on two shabby wicker chairs. One corner is occupied by a pale young mother and her three children. The two little girls lie sound asleep on their own camp beds, for this is a spacious shelter. Close to them the baby sleeps in his perambulator. For fear he may get the benefit of any stray breeze which by chance enters this airless cavern, he is wrapped in a thick rough blanket with the waterproof hood of the perambulator pulled up over his head.

We leave the inhabitants of the shelter to the relaxation which a sense of security gives them, and return to the post. On the way there we see two figures standing over a recumbent form in a lighted open doorway.

"Look here!" calls my friend. "You mustn't show that light!"

"I'm sorry, missus," comes the reply, "but someone's just took bad."

"Any help wanted? There are two wardens here."

"No, thank you. She's with 'er friends."

"Been on the razzle," the warden remarks aside to me.

At the post we find that a yellow warning ("Unlock shelters") has been on for two hours, but is now withdrawn. After so many successive nights of sirens, guns, and distant bombs, the quiet is unbelievable. It is too incredible to be reassuring.

"What's That Man up to now?" we ask each other, as our eyes search the inscrutable heavens for a plane or a flare, and our ears listen for the familiar hiccuping hum ten thousand feet above the barrage balloons. But the mysterious silence gives us no indication of That Man's intentions, and still less of those entertained by the Lord and Giver of Life, whose celestial floor is now the source of the unleashed death which explodes upon a helpless population.

After a short period of desultory conversation we doze for two hours in our chairs, while the men stretch themselves on mattresses in the cloak-room where the gas-proof suits are stored.

"Well," remarks my friend as we share a cup of tea with the other wardens on duty at seven A.M., "we'll have to ask you back again. You've brought us the first quiet night that we've had this week."

It is a bright crisp morning, vivid with early autumn sunshine. I decide to walk through West Kensington back to my home. Half an hour later, the first siren of the new day greets me when I am five minutes away from my own front door. I walk on at a steady pace, and reach it just as the heavy drone of the Nazi bomber throbs overhead.

18. LONDON UNDER FIRE

JUST BEFORE MIDNIGHT on a late August Saturday, Martin and I sit in our Chelsea dining-room drinking tea and contemplating bed. He gets up to put the last edition of the evening paper into the basket, when a sudden series of distant crashes cause us to stand still, listening. Almost immediately the siren wails, and we go downstairs into the air-raid shelter. We are hardly there when the Nazi raiders, like enormous malevolent mosquitoes, whine above the river. A few seconds later, a dull sickening thud shakes the eighteenth century house whose beauty-loving builders never contemplated the threat of mechanised warfare to its flat, clean-lined windows and graceful balustrades. The sound suggests hundreds of tea-trays falling downstairs or huge cartloads of coal being tipped into cellars.

Robert's friend, the air-raid warden from the block of flats opposite, calls to us as we look cautiously at the dark sky from the basement.

"Hear that? It was a screaming bomb they dropped. I heard it from the Embankment."

"Where was it? It sounded as near as Westminster."

"Bit further than that, I think. More like Ludgate Hill."

Robert scrambles up the area steps; then, excitedly, he calls down to us.

"You there, madam? Come out for a moment—they're not over just now. . . . Look at the sky!"

We struggle up the dark steps, and walk over to the Embankment. The night seems cool and fresh after the stuffy cellar; a smell of moist earth and damp leaves comes from the Embankment Gardens. Above the heavy late summer trees, the waning moon, like a Chinese lantern turned sideways, lights up the black vault spangled with stars. But is it only the moon?

Suddenly we turn and see, to the east, the ominous glow of fire creeping up the sky. Indifferent to raiders, we run upstairs to the top floor balcony, but the house on the corner cuts off the view. We go down and, again hurrying across the road, lean anxiously over the river parapet. To the north of the Thames, the sky above the City resembles a flaming sunset. As we watch with a cold sensation in the pit of our stomach, the drone of the raiders sounds overhead, high above the clouds and the balloon barrage which protects us from dive-bombers and prevents the invader from recognising his objective. Once more safety seems more desirable than experience, and we hasten indoors.

The time is now 1.30 A.M. For two hours the raid has continued; the glow in the sky is slowly dying away. The bursts of intermittent gunfire have also ceased; over the night, like a suffocating coverlet, lies that sinister silence, characteristic of all raid periods free from noise, which makes us feel that a large number of unpleasant occurrences are happening somewhere else. . . .

We decide to go to bed, and have just undressed when the all-clear begins in the distance. I turn out the light, pull back the curtains, and lean out of the window. At first the sound is far away, starting from the raided City; then, as one London district after another takes it up, it comes gradually nearer until at last the great siren on the Embankment roars in our ears. Sighing with relief, I turn on the bath-water; even growing familiarity with raid-warnings has not yet removed my reluctance to take a bath when at any moment the bombs may descend.

We are just getting into bed when a sudden series of detonations comes from the distance.

"Listen!" I call to Martin. "The guns again!"

But there is no further sound. In the morning I shall realise that the noise came from explosions wrecking offices and stores in the neighbourhood of St. Paul's—St. Paul's which is to become, it seems, a major air-raid objective. Now, whatever further terrors this night may have, I am too stupefied with fatigue to care. I fall asleep, and sleep like the dead—the dead in the City. . . .

We Londoners shall not be long in learning that this Saturday night was only a beginning. In the next fortnight, London has thirty raids, and her citizens visit department stores in thousands to purchase mattresses and campbeds for their inadequate shelters. Gradually they become accustomed to nightly descents into the basement, and dawn trips back to their bedrooms after the sound of the all-clear. We believe we are discovering how well we can manage with a few hours' sleep—or none.

At present, since only a few districts have suffered, there is no rushing to shelters when the sirens begin, though one morning the sight of an old man dropping dead in front of Kensington Cinema at the first banshee note makes me realise the secret terror with which it is awaited by the elderly and helpless.

"Don't hurry, dearie!" urges a woman walking quietly

towards a shelter to an agitated old lady on a Sunday afternoon. "It's not the raid, it's the hurryin' that upsets you."

In London omnibuses the conversation now becomes general and turns wholly upon air-raids.

"It's them that are careless what get it," remarks the conductor of a bus running from the Euston Road through Shaftesbury Avenue. "You sh'd see 'em walkin' home from Hampstead Heath with cigarettes in their mouths—and me in a place where I can't take cover! Got to be on duty at eight in the morning, too."

"Well," comments a girl passenger, "I got so tired waiting in the shelter last night I started to walk back—but I kept my eyes and ears open, and every time I heard gun-fire I dived under cover. It's not such a nice walk in the middle of the night."

"Not it," agrees the conductor. "What I says is, it's not just what they throw down—it's when they swoop down. It's *right* for the likes of me to go into the shelters. Then, when the all-clear goes, I'm there with the bus to take the people home."

In the theatres and concert halls, impromptu perform-ances now follow the programmes to fill the time during six- and seven-hour raids. After a few days, most people continue their occupations when the siren sounds; often, writing my book or dictating letters, I become so oblivious of the raid that when the all-clear goes, I imagine it to be another warning. In some of the big stores, "roof-spotters" now relay a running commentary to the customers taking shelter below.

"There's a puff of smoke in the north-west. . . . Now there's nothing, so I'll put on a record."

A famous contributor to a widely read daily newspaper

quotes a correspondent who tells him that the New York newspapers used such heavy type for their headlines during the preliminary raids on Britain that, now the real Blitzkrieg is arriving, they have no further resources left. Their situation, he says, reminds him of an old-time St. Louis editor, who found on returning from a holiday that his deputy had used the big type which he believed he had locked up for an emergency.

"You idiot!" he shouted. "Don't you know I was keeping that for the Second Coming of our Lord!"

The only persons who suffer from London's half-amused indifference to raiders are the air-raid wardens, who cannot take cover until others have done so. But even the sang-froid of the capital's workers will not continue for many more days. A time is coming when no type ever invented will satisfy the American newspapers. Already, if we are honest, we shall admit that we wake every morning with heads heavy and eyes dry from the interrupted night; that the daily sirens are beginning to challenge our powers of concentration with their insistent scream. But whether we wanted the war or not, whether we worked for it or against it, we are universally determined that it shall not get us down. Doggedly we continue our daily occupations, though we know that what we are doing cannot possibly be our best. Some of us, too, constantly remember the young men sentenced by the blunders and inertia of past politicians to the ordeal of perpetual vigilance at aerodromes and searchlight batteries.

Each morning, when daylight re-illumines the scene which at night has appeared so menacing, we look carefully round to see whether any familiar landmark has disappeared. This abnormal life has come to resemble a diabolical game of musical chairs—a game in which we continually wonder whether we shall be near our destination when the siren goes, and give way to a sigh of relief each time an absent member of the household walks safely in at the garden gate.

On August 30th, Martin is obliged to leave England for America in order to fulfil a university contract made the previous winter when Hitler was still behind the Maginot Line. Even before he leaves, the Nazi raiders have come to Chelsea. One night, when we are halfway up our tall house, they sound so close above us that I want to duck my head. In less than a second, my blood is chilled by a descending scream—a scream so often described by friends and in war-books that I recognise it immediately, though I have never heard it before.

"Did you hear that?" I call to Martin. "It sounded like a bomb just outside the window!"

We listen tensely, waiting for the house to shake, perhaps to fall. Nothing happens.

"It can't have been a bomb," says Martin at last. We go to bed—he upstairs, I, more cautiously, in the coal-cellar. Next morning we learn that two delayed-action bombs have fallen in the square a hundred yards from our house where Richard and Hilary used to play.

Martin, unhappy and reluctant, is nevertheless compelled to sail for America. He takes with him a large box of oil-paints for Richard and a collection of velvet animals for Hilary, bought in Kensington, to make up for the leaving presents that I never gave. I see him off at Euston on his way to the north. He leaves at 4.50 P.M. in the midst of an air-raid, and does not arrive at his destination until the next day. Now that raids are spread all over the country, the night-trains travel cautiously for fear of "incidents" or "mishaps" on the line.

When Martin has gone and I am left to contemplate the Blitzkrieg with all my family overseas, London herself becomes my companion. Never, it seems to me, has she looked so beautiful as during these hours when she faces an ordeal the like of which she has never known through the centuries of her history. Outside the windows of our lonely house, the Thames from Westminster to Putney coils like a shining serpent basking in sunshine. At night the stars, so clearly visible in the black-out, appear as a million diamonds scattered upon a cushion of deep blue velvet. When I go to spend a few days with a friend at her little Queen Anne house in an old Kensington square, the borders and circular beds in the public garden are aflame with dahlias and geraniums which rival, with their orange and scarlet, the fires that light the midnight sky after the fall of incendiary bombs. It is as though the old city were consciously putting on her loveliest aspect in order to ask her citizens to endure for her sake.

On the afternoon of the first Saturday in September, I am invited to attend a conference in Oxford Street. Going home, I decide to walk through the Park from Marble Arch to Hyde Park Corner, and cannot understand why the Saturday crowd is gathered in little expectant groups outside the huts and shelters. Suddenly, as I emerge from the gateway opposite St. George's Hospital, London is shaken by the roar of guns, and, looking up, I see twelve Nazi aeroplanes almost above us with puffs of shrapnel bursting around them.

"Why, it's a raid!" I exclaim unnecessarily to a fellow-spectator. "The siren never went, did it?"

"It did, though—half an hour or more ago," she replies, and I realise that the clamour of our conference must have drowned even its wail. After a moment's hesitation, for the battle has its grim excitement, I take a taxi to Kensington, and from the roof of my friend's house watch heavy columns of smoke pouring skywards from the direction of the docks.

The dockyard fire burns all evening; it is not in fact extinguished for two days. At nightfall, after we have drawn the curtains, it lights up London with midday brilliance for the benefit of the Nazi raiders who fly citywards in their hundreds for the first night of the intensified Blitzkrieg. My friend and I are not aware of it; instead, we are listening, startled, to the unfamiliar ringing of church bells, and wondering whether the threatened invasion has begun. But the evening siren has just sounded when the young Esthonian maid peeps through the curtains of the first-floor drawing-room.

"Oh, look! Fire! How red the sky! Do come and see."

I am just turning to look, when a blow such as I have never known even in nightmares seems to strike the house like a gigantic flail. I am swept off my feet and out of my senses; somehow, a second later, I find myself in the basement, but even before I arrive there a second terrific crash makes the whole earth rock like a ship in mountainous seas. The cook, already below, tells us later that the house appeared to gather itself up and pitch forward; for a moment she thought that we were all going to be flung into the road from above her head. The blast has blown glass from the leaded panes, though the windows were open; sulphur fumes, thick and acrid, pour through the passages; an hour or so later, from the pricking of my reddened skin, I realise that something has scorched my face.

Gathering myself up from the basement, I go to the telephone with the abnormal calm that for most of us follows an escape from death before the reaction begins:

"Is that the Kensington police? Look here, when the raid's over you'd better come and take a glance at 37, Francis Square. We've either had a bomb on our roof, or it's fallen just outside. I don't know how much damage there is, but the whole house seemed to be coming on top of us."

A few minutes later the police arrive; the raid is still on, but they know that it will not be over till dawn. As they plunge ankle-deep in glass to look for damage with their shrouded torches, they tell me that seven bombs fell in three seconds within a quarter of a mile of our house. Eventually they discover that the bomb which so nearly demolished us has fallen and exploded, not upon our roof, but upon that of the house in an adjoining crescent which backs on to ours. Amazingly, a woman who was having a bath on the second floor has escaped with no more than shock.

Sitting in the basement when the police have gone, holding a cup of tea in hands now ignobly shaking, I reflect that shock is quite bad enough. Wondering whether my face is as green as the faces of the others, I contemplate with astonishment the fact that I am still alive.

19. ANNIVERSARY

On Tuesday September 3, 1940, the first anniversary of the Second World War, there is a raid warning—the thirty-second since August 15th—at 10.30 a.m. It lasts till 11.30—precisely a year from the first pseudo-warning which sounded over London immediately after Neville Chamberlain had broadcast the declaration of war. The siren to-day is no fake alarm; all morning, from the misty blue-grey ceiling, comes the throb of invisible aeroplanes—the British light, the German dull and heavy. Whatever part of London we live in, they always seem, by day or by night, to be passing just overhead.

As soon as the all-clear has gone, the now familiar queue of interrupted shoppers appears in the stores. All the taxicabs are speedily snapped up by people caught far from their homes, so that five minutes after a raid is over, motor transport is unobtainable. The post-offices, which still close during raids, are crowded with buyers of stamps and senders of parcels; the mailbags pile up in the sorting-office, and telephone calls and telegrams are "heavily delayed."

At the headquarters of a peace-organisation where I often work, I find one of my colleagues distressed because the parents of a friend are air-raid casualties in a Yorkshire coast town.

"Denis's mother was killed, and his father had his arm blown off," he tells me sadly. "The Nazi machine was brought down, and when Denis went to see his mother in the mortuary, her body was lying beside the bodies of the four German airmen who had bombed her house."

When the disturbed morning has ended, and a second afternoon warning is over with one of the hottest days of this grimly beautiful summer, London looks up in the late evening to a perfect pale blue sky, with feathery drifts of cloud sweeping like celestial brooms across the peaceful heavens from which death and disaster so incongruously descend. To my now preoccupied imagination, the rooks flying home resemble miniature black bombers, strangely menacing in their flight. But away to the west, a luminous cirrus-cloud formation takes on the appearance of a distant seashore with snow-white sands, where tired humanity, wearied of the terrible futility of destruction, may rest at last. Perhaps, I reflect, that placid evening sky after hours of battle is symbolic of the life of my generation. Perhaps, when the too eventful days of our years have drawn nearer to their close, we who have known so much war and catastrophe will find peace at eventide.

All over this lovely island which peril has rendered dearer than ever to us all, we look upon the same warm harvest beauty which greeted the outbreak of war a year ago. But there are desolate areas now—London districts with houses, streets, or factories demolished; seaside towns and ports with acres of ruin behind a proud façade of normality; damaged regions in Wales, Scotland, the Midlands, and the West. There is little, perhaps, which as yet rivals France's devastated areas in 1915, but at last we in England know war as it has not appeared here since the Civil War four hundred years ago, nor from outside these shores for nearly nine centuries.

When I walk a hundred yards from my Chelsea house and inspect the craters made by the time-bombs in the pleasant square where the children played as babies, I realise that war now appears to me much as it looked to the mothers of France and Belgium twenty-five years ago. We need not, as I did then, put on a uniform and take a train and boat in order to find it. In spite of the still normal appearance of most homes and gardens, of the household routine which—for how much longer?—we refuse to allow raid warnings to disturb, the war is always with us whether we want it or not. We endeavour to defeat its influence by going steadily on with our job— whether this be guarding an aerodrome, working in an office or factory, tending patients in hospital, cooking the dinner, or writing a book—with the maximum concentration of which we are capable. The better we wrest order out of potential chaos, the more effectively we counter, not merely the attacking Nazis, but war itself.

Sometimes, in the midst of this determined self-discipline, we pause to think—a function which even those of us who are accustomed to attempt it will certainly perform more effectively when, if ever, the present period of sleepless nights and interrupted days recedes into the past. When we do succeed in concentrating our minds upon recent events, we realise what a year of history lies behind us: a twelvemonth of almost uninterrupted calamity. We remember the invasions of Poland, Finland, Norway, Denmark, Holland, and Belgium; the collapse of France like a mammoth tree eaten away at the roots; the astonishing rescue of the British Expeditionary Force from annihilation at Dunkirk; the change of government at Westminster after the Norwegian evacuation; the air fights over Kent, Essex, and London. We recall the galloping sequence of events which has left us alone to carry on a war that need never have occurred if our statesmen had been ready to show the same unsupported courage at the council tables of Europe as this nation is now displaying on the battlefields of Britain.

How many of us reflect that, hitherto, history has recorded man's disasters rather than the tale of his constructive achievements? "Happy is the country that has no history" is an aphorism taken by most of us to mean, "How fortunate is the nation which has had no calamities to interrupt the story of its progress!" I remember lecturing at Middlesbrough on the evening of Edward VIII's abdication, and remarking that, like most of my audience, I belonged to a generation which had known too much history in the accepted sense of the word. How much more we were still to experience, I did not then realise—although, having visited Germany that spring and heard Hitler speak at Cologne on the eve of the election which followed the Nazi march into the Rhineland, I perceived possibilities which I hoped that Europe's politicians might still have the belated wisdom to forestall.

Now we are right in the midst of an epoch which for tragedy and intensity has probably never been equalled. Whatever our occupations and opinions, we tend, with each day of isolated struggle, to become more and more consciously citizens of this land.

It is not the anniversary of the war itself, but the following Sunday, which has been appointed as a day of national rededication to whatever ideal of service each individual may pursue. A night of terrible bombing has followed the onslaught upon Kensington which almost wrecked my friend's house, and we realise that the aerial Blitzkrieg has entered a new phase which is going to make fresh demands upon the endurance of us who imagined that we knew, by now, what air-raids meant.

Going out in the early morning to inspect the damage caused by the seven bombs that fell upon our district, I wish with all my heart that I possessed a better endowment of natural courage with which to face the ordeal before us. Feeling cold in the pale morning sunshine after the shock of last night's bomb-blast, I try to reconstruct, from the scene of ruin before me, the former appearance of the wide, pleasant avenue whose houses run parallel, back to back, with those on my friend's side of Francis Square. Why, I wonder vaguely, did I go to Wimbledon to look for damage, when I had only to wait a few days before it came to me? Most of the windows have vanished from the backs of the Francis Square houses, but in Worcester Gardens there is hardly a door unwrenched, a window frame untwisted. The squalor of destruction has made a temporary slum of these once prosperous middle-class homes. As I walk past the little crowd which stands gazing, open-mouthed, at the gruesome transformation, the sound of a hymn from a church near by mingles oddly with the chink of broken glass as it is gathered by street-cleaners and air-raid wardens from roads and gardens.

Later, in the church of St. Martin-in-the-Fields where Winifred Holtby's memorial service was held and Dick Sheppard used to preach, I stare dazedly at the gold-embossed blue ceiling while the Rev. Pat McCormick, himself already face to face with death, thanks God for "the essential honour, fairness, and decency of the British spirit." America, we learn, is praying for us to-day at President Roosevelt's request. Thinking of her—but not of her only—we stand up and sing the hymn, "These things shall be":

> Nation with nation, land with land,
> Unarmed shall live as comrades free;
> In every heart and brain shall throb
> The pulse of one fraternity.

After such a night, it is difficult to avoid falling asleep on one's knees; more difficult still to follow the preacher's address on prayer, though his plea for "the wounded, suffering, bereaved, and homeless" is one of which more and more British men and women will stand in need in the days to come. I look round the congregation and see the greying heads, the lined faces, of men and women who, twenty-five years ago, prayed as the victims of war once prayed before Troy that their God might not be angry for ever ... Never, perhaps, has an English generation suffered so much as the one that was born in the closing years of the nineteenth century—a century which, in the unparalleled speed of its material achievements, had lost the spiritual resilience which alone can rescue the race of man from its tendency to self-destruction. But if, when this Second Great War of our lifetime is over, we can weave from the stuff of our experience a pattern of civilisation quite other than the stereotyped design which formed the background of our youth, perhaps we may even find it to have been expedient that one generation should suffer for posterity.

The congregation is standing; the last verse of the final hymn swells from the organ to remind us of the double purpose to which our lives, while they last, must be dedicated:

O beautiful, our country!
Round thee in love we draw;
Thine is the grace of freedom,
The majesty of law.
Be righteousness thy sceptre,
Justice thy diadem;
And on thy shining forehead
Be peace the crowning gem.

As we emerge from the church with the reiterated summons of Blake's "Jerusalem" echoing in our ears, the siren wails once more over London. The buses fill; taxicabs hasten to the door of St. Martin's; a few members of the congregation, their night's experiences too vivid for the immediate return of equanimity, hurry down to the shelter of the crypt.

Peace! Will it ever return? O Lover of Concord, how long?

20. THE TRAINING CENTRES CARRY ON

IN THIS WAR which has become a struggle of production versus production rather than of men versus men, the British government has found it necessary to start a number of training centres for the expansion of wartime labour.

The engineering trade in particular is growing daily, since "munitions" includes every requirement of war in addition to the death-dealing and damage-inflicting weapons which are now the major objects of industry. Lorries, signalling sets, searchlights, the very tools themselves, all become "munitions" in wartime, and their additional makers are recruited from "non-essential" industries.

By September, 1940, there are seventeen centres in Great Britain training men as semi-skilled engineers, with a total of over twelve thousand places, and the Ministry of Labour hopes soon to have enough centres to train one hundred thousand a year. The trades taught to the trainees include draughtsmanship, fitting, instrument making, machine operating, panel beating and sheet metal working, and electric and oxyacetylene welding. In addition to the training centres, a number of colleges and polytechnics already in existence have undertaken to provide training courses for the Ministry of Labour and national service.

When a friend in the government asks me if I should like to inspect a training centre for women, I decide to go. Although I am hardly an ideal reporter of munition-making and its purpose, I am interested in discovering just what are the "non-essential" occupations from which the would-be munition workers are recruited. I suspect that, as always in war, it is those trades and professions which create the beauty, the grace, and the culture of civilised living, which will have been sacrificed in order that the present objectives of inflicting death and perpetrating destruction may be maintained with maximum ferocity. Once a modern society has chosen war as its final method of resolving its differences with its antagonist, it must look forward to a period in which life approximates ever more closely to human existence in primitive communities, as described by the seventeenth-century philosopher Thomas Hobbes: "solitary, poore, nasty, brutish and short."

It is the 9th of September. The second night of the full-scale Blitzkrieg has been one of the worst that we shall endure; bombs and aerial torpedoes have fallen every five minutes for a period of ten hours, dropped by groups of apparently unintercepted raiders who have circled the metropolis at least twenty times. Trying to rest in our fragile basement, with a cushion over my face to save my head from the expected descent of the ceiling, I have listened to bombs dropping nearer and nearer from each group of raiders, waited tensely for the next to fall on me, and relaxed twenty times for a few moments when the crash has sounded just on the hither side. For the second successive period after nearly four weeks of interrupted nights, I have not slept at all. Now I nod in the taxicab on my way to the Ministry of Labour, though London has at last begun to display recognisable wounds, and each ugly gap in a familiar street strikes with the effect of a new blow upon the most bemused imagination.

At the Ministry I talk for half an hour to a friendly official, who explains to me some of the changes now occurring within the munitions industry. Even in peacetime, he tells me, the engineering profession is among the largest in the country and, within limits, is one of the most skilled. The highly trained operators who "set" their own machines amount only to about twenty thousand; the mass of workers use machines which others have set up. One of the chief processes now going on, I learn, is known as "de-skilling"; a job which in peacetime can be done by one experienced man is divided between several so that each operation requires a smaller measure of skill.

I put the question that I am most anxious to have answered: "What are the chief occupations which are regarded as non-essential in wartime?"

"Well," replies the official, "we can easily make one list by considering the industries where unemployment already exists. There are all the luxury trades, of course—clothing and dressmaking, and the whole field of cosmetics and beauty treatment, which had come to be one of the biggest. Then there's the seaside hotel industry, which now has a great deal of unemployment, particularly since the East and South coasts were made into defence areas. Jewellery is another hard-hit occupation, though a good many employees have got government contracts because they're accustomed to fine work, and are particularly useful, for instance, at joining up the various parts of small instruments. Then there are a large number of printers out of work owing to the restrictions on paper. And the building trade is suffering, except for repairs."

"I should have thought it would soon be having a field day, if the raids go on as they are."

"Well, as I say, people are having essential repairs done, like boarding up windows and doors, and propping up unsafe structures. But nobody's going to have a house rebuilt while it may be bombed again."

"There'd be plenty of work for builders," I suggest, "if the government provided deep shelters for the population of London—as they've so often been asked to do."

"Yes, of course—but there are certain difficulties. . . ."

"It's going to be hell in the East End if this bombardment goes on. There ought to be no difficulties in the way of preventing that."

He does not pursue the subject, and I put my next inquiry.

"What about the human side of this transfer business? How do people like changing over from a job in which they are well qualified to another where they have to start all over again?"

"Some of them seem to enjoy it, as you'll see. We do find a certain amount of resentment, of course, particularly from workers who are not accustomed to standing up all day."

"And what about the women? Do they always get the lighter work to do—and the less well-paid?"

"Well—that's the general custom, but you do find places where it's just the opposite. In Birmingham, for instance, a number of women have taken on work which is too dirty for the men, because that's the tradition. If you'll

come along with me now to the south of the river, you'll
see how women who have done quite different jobs are
being trained as munition workers."

We drive through debris and past barricaded streets
which increase as we approach the Embankment, to a
famous institute in Lambeth, built nearly a century ago
by a local family. Once a junior technical school for about
one hundred and forty boys, it was taken over before the
war by the Women's Engineering Society as a training
centre for women engineers. The three hundred women
who now attend have no fee to pay; they even receive
their fares and a maintenance allowance. As soon as they
are trained, they come into the common labour pool and
are placed where the Ministry most needs workers.

Only a few of the trainees are here this morning, for
the sudden intensification of air-raids has dislocated London's transport. Trams, buses, and Underground railways
are all in process of adapting themselves to "emergencies"
which officialdom has hitherto regarded as normal for
Pekin, Madrid, Warsaw, Helsinki, Oslo, Rotterdam, and
even Paris, but quite unlikely really to occur in London.
As everyone who has worked in a government department
knows, the readjustment of the official mind is at least as
exacting a proposition as the speedy repair of damaged
railways and tramlines. Meanwhile, it is only the trainees
who can afford taxis, possess bicycles, or live near enough
to the training centre to get there on their feet, who are
able to arrive at their work even approximately near the
hour when the day's instruction begins.

We walk round the workshop and talk to some of the
women already employed there. A girl who once worked
at Harrod's, and the ex-proprietress of a dressmaking

establishment in South Molton Street, are each engaged in making a plumb-bob. An actress who belonged to a repertory company has come on her bicycle from Putney Hill, making her way past burst gas and water mains along the Embankment. She is busy—and, it seems, very happy —constructing a spanner.

"Just why do you like it so much?" I inquire.

She meditates, a little puzzled.

"I don't know. I never thought of asking myself. I suppose it's the fascination of seeing something solid emerge."

A girl who calls herself "just a married woman" nods in agreement.

"I find I can do things with my hands I never even thought of. That's what I like."

In another room where the trainees are learning to make drawings to scale, I find an ex-student of Economics from Cambridge who intended to become a probation officer.

"I'm interested in trying to connect up the two jobs," she tells me. "There's some sort of controlled planning scheme dawning in my mind in which they're both equally relevant. That's as far as I've got at present."

After talking to an admiral's sister, a nursery-school teacher, a maker of art pottery, and a student from the London School of Economics, I am at last taken to the woman superintendent, who has just arrived after three hours' travelling from a much-bombed area on the edge of south-east London.

This institute, she tells me, is the only one in the South of England doing work of its kind.

"We started from scratch on June 3rd with thirty trainees. Now we have about two hundred working by day, and another hundred in the evenings. Most of them had good jobs of various kinds before the war."

"I was talking to some of them upstairs," I tell her. "Do they all enjoy the change of work as much as the ones I saw?"

"Oh, we have our tragedies, of course. There was one woman who never got over losing her teaching job in Budapest and her lovely flat above the Danube. Another was a lecturer at the British Institute in Paris. To see her trying to settle down to filing is either amusing or pathetic, according to the way you look at it."

"How far do most of them take it up purely as war work—from patriotism or a sense of duty?"

"Not all of them, by any means. We've got one girl, the wife of a pilot, who thoroughly resents the war and isn't specially anxious to help the country. When she came here she said to me: 'I've got to have a routine in my life.' She finds this training a means of personal salvation just because it gives her a regular job."

After I have left, the woman superintendent sends me a list of the occupations previously followed by the trainees at the institute. I read it through with some curiosity: "Office workers, 58; housewife or no specified occupation, 138; dressmaker, milliner, tailor, 21; cutter or designer, 7; saleswoman, 23; teacher, 16; journalist, 13; beauty specialist, 11; supervisor, 14; artist, 10; actress, 8; catering or domestic, 17; A.R.P., 8; nurse, 5."

They are revealing figures. I suspect that, had we tabulated the previous occupations of the would-be escorts at the Children's Overseas Reception Board, the proportions would not have been dissimilar. In peacetime we are told that the housewife is the cornerstone of that family unity which is the moral foundation of English life, but in wartime she becomes a person "of no specified occupation," who counts no more than the family unity which is itself one of the first casualties of modern war.

Teachers, I realise, though still essential, may have been left behind when a particular school was evacuated to the country with a reduced staff, while the journalists are probably the persevering unsuccessful free-lances of peacetime, and not the skilled reporters whose experience and intrepidity are at a premium in war. But why nurses? I wonder, recalling the incessant demand for nursing Sisters and Red Cross auxiliaries in the last Great War.

Then I remember that these reflections are twenty-five years out of date. In this war, despite Dunkirk, our casualties have been machines and supplies rather than men; hence we still have waiting lists of nurses who are and will probably remain unemployed. A few more may be called up as the air-raid casualties increase, but even then, though thousands of innocent men, women, and children will die, it will be houses, offices, and public buildings which need restoration in larger quantities than human beings. To-day, though machines are destroying a civilisation, we shall not repeat the epoch in which men's vulnerable bodies were flung in their millions against fire and steel, as at Passchendaele and for years on the Somme.

21. COUNTRY VISIT, STYLE 1940

AFTER FOUR WEEKS of continuous bombing, the prospect
of three days in a Surrey town seems to offer a welcome
break. It will not, we know, give security—no place in the
Home Counties can now be relied on for that—but at least
we shall have freedom from perpetual noise and the
blessed opportunity of a nightly sleep.

So my friend and I accept the invitation. It is difficult
to reach Waterloo, for a bomb has recently fallen on
the route, but after a prolonged series of detours, we
drive up the station approach. The great terminus is
shrouded in a suspicious quietness. One or two porters
stand, with folded arms, at the entrance to the deserted
platforms.

Our innocent inquiry about the next train to W. is
treated with scorn.

"You can't get nowhere from here. Station's closed."

"Do you mean to say I can't get to W. at all?"

"The only way's round by the suburbs. We're shut down
here till further notice."

Determined not to miss our peaceful nights, which now
seem more desirable than ever, we tell the taxi-driver to
go on to the suburban station. After a long drive past the
now customary railed-off roads and heaps of broken glass,

we are stopped outside Clapham by a youth in the uniform of the Home Guards.

"I'm sorry, but you can't go further than this. There's trouble on the line, and we've got orders to stop everyone here.

"But they told us at Waterloo that trains to W. were running from this station."

"The trains are running, but you go at your own risk. I can help you with your luggage if you like."

We get out of the taxi, and the young man carries our cases across the road. Outside the booking office, I wait in a long queue while a distracted clerk issues tickets to distant destinations seldom asked for at this suburban station. I have just succeeded in getting ours, when the familiar wail starts overhead.

"Air-raid warning! Passengers are advised to take cover in the station shelter."

We decide to go on. A train comes in that will carry us at least part of the way to the town which is usually a swift forty minutes run from London, and to continue our journey seems hardly more of a risk than to remain in a station where a time-bomb may explode at any moment.

Twenty minutes later, after the train has stopped continually between Clapham and Wimbledon, we wonder whether we have chosen wisely, for we suddenly hear the sound of an aerial battle overhead. As always during an air-raid, the blinds of the train windows are drawn, but when we stop at Berrylands Park, we see the alighting passengers run for their lives. Lifting the blind, we watch incendiary bombs dropping like tennis balls on the roads near the railway line, and listen, with a horrid pricking of our hair, to machine-gun bullets rattling on the carriage roof.

"Better get down," our male travelling companion advises grimly.

Without ceremony, we flatten ourselves amid the dust and cigarette ends on the carriage floor as again the train begins to move. This time, I conclude, my last moment *must* have come. Why wasn't I endowed with a greater share of native intrepidity, since I have to exist in days like these?

But the small train, miraculously unhit, moves steadily along. At the large station where we have to change, an insecure above-ground shelter offers cover of a kind, but now we are beyond the reach of the Nazi planes surging towards London. A fast train to W. suddenly arrives on the opposite platform and, trembling with relief, we climb in. Just before we reach our destination, the all-clear echoes from the distance. We arrive at W. after three hours of perilous travel.

Compared with London, this dormitory town gives an impression of suburban normality, but it is crowded, uncomfortable, and noisy. Like most country towns within a few miles of London, it is filled with troops and thronged with evacuees. Every night, the German bombers drone heavily towards the capital, occasionally flinging haphazard bombs over the little two-storey houses and bungalows which have no shelters or basements for refuge. At dawn they return, to release any further bombs which the ferocity of the London barrage has compelled them to carry away.

The first night we sleep soundly, driven by accumulated fatigue to an abysmal indifference towards bombers and their loads. But on the next, as the sullen intermittent hum sounds overhead, we begin our too familiar speculations.

Will the next sporadic outbreak of bursting bombs descend on our heads?

Throughout the third night, the continuous sound of violent gunfire echoes from London's newly strengthened defences. Here, thirty miles from the centre of the city, we have a grandstand position for watching the furious barrage; but as the swift succession of shells breaks in the sky with scarlet flashes like some colossal firework display above the greenish light of the bursting bombs, we decide that we prefer being inside the barrage to being behind it. Peace, perhaps, may still be sought on the shores of the Cumberland lakes, in the mountains of North Wales, or along the deep red lanes of Devon, but within the precincts of London there is only war.

Next day we return to the city by car. Though rain is falling heavily, we run into an air-raid before we are out of Surrey. Bombs are dropping on Fulham and Kensington as the car makes its hazardous way between piles of glass, and winds backwards and forwards through the few remaining roads which are not barricaded. I drive straight to a service flat which I have taken temporarily in the West End, for Robert's young wife has already left for the country with her baby, and Robert is following her as soon as arrangements can be made at the other end. The large house on the Embankment—too unwieldy to be managed under air-raid conditions for the benefit of a solitary female—must be closed until more normal days return.

As I reach the entrance to the block of flats, the anti-aircraft guns are barking loudly; another fierce aerial battle is in progress over London. I stand watching the rainy sky for the fighting planes, when suddenly, from behind a low concealing cloud, three huge German bombers dive towards the flats and seem to be making straight for me. Without further recklessness I run ignominiously to the basement, where lunch is already laid in the underground dining-room. Sitting down to eat it, I meditate with shame on the process of adaptation which enables a peace-loving citizen to enjoy a meal while men are fighting for their lives overhead.

I am not, however, permitted to enjoy it long, for a call summons me to the telephone-booth on the ground floor. Robert, hastily evacuating himself to a relative at the other end of London, reports that a time-bomb has just fallen within a few yards of our Chelsea house. The police, he tells me, have forbidden us to go near it again until the explosion has occurred.

22. BRITISH MORALE

DURING THE WEEKS which have passed since the Battle for
Britain began, those of us who live in London, on the
coast, or in major industrial cities, have watched from near
or far the fiercest and most momentous aerial battles that
modern history has ever known.

In smoke and flame the most highly trained young airmen of two nations have fallen from the sky, and with
them a youthful American, gay, fortunate, brilliant, an
only son whose best years should have lain before him.
However daring and heroic these boys may be, any one
of us who possesses imagination can picture the emotions
that they endure before each of their swift, intense flights.

By sea and land, co-operating with the Air Force, our
sailors are watching the sinister waters which protect us,
dodging bombs and torpedoes, convoying vital cargoes;
our anti-aircraft gunners and searchlight batteries are
standing by continually under fire. This island is filled
with regiments holding perilous positions, and boys on
duty at aerodromes which are main targets of enemy
bombers.

Even this is not the end. Never, I suppose, has the sum
total of civilian courage in this country proved so great
as it is to-day in response to the intense and perpetual

strain placed upon it. This courage is not even confined to the civilian defence forces, those ordinary men and women in steel hats who patrol the streets during raids, fight fires, rescue casualties from the debris of buildings, and lay down their lives at first-aid posts. Day after day, men and women working in offices, in factories, or in their own homes, fight their human fears with a brave show of cheerful indifference. Even the children sing in their shelters, subjecting themselves prematurely to adult self-control—with what long-range effects on their nervous systems, we do not yet know.

In addition to the raids which now occur six or seven times a day and finally continue throughout the night, the inhabitants of London and the South-Eastern counties face the possibility of shells and rockets being dropped on their houses and streets. Dover has been shelled continually; no one can guess how soon some long-range monster may join the bombs, and aerial torpedoes which fall on Greater London. At any moment, death may descend upon any one of us from the brilliant noonday skies or the serene moonlit clouds. The people of Britain are learning to confront fate with a heroism which is none the less magnificent because it is universal.

Some years ago, when he still described himself as a pacifist, Dr. C. E. M. Joad defined civilian morale as "the willingness to die quietly." In those days his epigram seemed witty and amusing. It is less amusing now, when hundreds of civilians, for no fault except that of failing to oppose with sufficient vigour the policy of weak provocation pursued by successive British governments, have suffered with precisely the measure of grim resigned patience that Dr. Joad foresaw.

We need not suppose that the courage and gaiety in

disaster so often publicised by the newspapers is invented
or exaggerated by a government-inspired Press. This type
of abnormal jubilation exists in all calamities. As most of
us who have been through crises of fear or sorrow know,
the first reaction when some dire experience has been survived is one of abnormal calm or hysterical cheerfulness.
I realised this anew on September 7th, just as I realised it
on many occasions twenty-five years ago; I also know how
acute is the reaction that sets in a day or two afterwards.
If people who have lost their homes, been blown up,
injured, burned, or buried were to be interviewed forty-
eight hours later, the results would not always be so useful
to the Sunshine Press.

Coupled with the astonishing courage which surrounds
us, the emotion that Amelia Earhart called "the livid lone-
liness of fear" is now also a universal experience. How
many men and women in this tiny country really listen
with indifference to the hiccuping boom of the Nazi
bomber as it passes overhead? The most conscientious of
war propagandists need not despise this secret terror.
Without it, "civilian morale" would not be the outstanding
achievement that it is. The conquest of fear—and to-day it
is conquered or effectively concealed by hundreds of thousands of decent citizens—is only the greater tribute to that
unquenchable vigour of the human spirit which a whole
nation displays.

And for what? We in Britain are growing so accustomed
to the demand made upon our endurance, our humour,
and our self-control that we have almost ceased to ask ourselves just why they are required. For what end is this
people showing its superlative courage? For what purpose
is it making, at incalculable cost, the emotional sacrifices
involved in parting with children, abandoning homes,

leaving husbands or wives in danger, closing down businesses, terminating professions, concluding social experiments which have embodied the hopes and dreams of a lifetime?

We are doing, permitting, and enduring these things in order that we may destroy another great nation whose airmen, soldiers, sailors, and civilians are also displaying superb gallantry and endurance. These virtues, we maintain, have been commandeered on false pretences; they are vainly sacrificed on the altar of a creed which maintains that there is no higher authority than the State. Believing, now, that force is the only method of extinguishing so false a doctrine, we have called upon our finest qualities in order that grief, terror, and despair may be inflicted not only upon a hostile government, but upon the unhappy people who accepted it. The outcome of our nobility can only be their greater suffering, their more prolonged ordeal.

It may be that now we have no alternative to pressing on to victory over the men and women who have endorsed and practised the militaristic creed which now forces us to perfect the arts of destruction. It may be that we can do nothing else than convert those conquered countries which were once our friends into starving hostages whose clamorous needs will cause them to rise against their conqueror. But I who so dearly love my country, and so deeply admire its brave imperturbable people, refuse to admit that I am joining the defeatists when I inquire what would have happened if all the energy, courage, and resourcefulness which is now dedicated to the work of destruction had been given to seeking a solution for Europe's problems while time still remained.

The question has its significance for the future. This

war, we say, was brought upon the world by one nation's ruthless ambition. Even supposing this simple analysis to be the truth, could not the national genius that we possess and are now displaying have suggested a policy which would have prevented the rise of those ambitious rulers, or a plan which would have compelled them to negotiate a tolerable peace in their own interests as well as ours? The aggressor, however cruel his methods and evil his intentions, is never solely to blame, since aggression must always prove abortive unless it is assisted from without by provocation, incompetence, indifference, or—as only too often within recent years—by all three combined.

Why must it be only in war that we awaken from our inertia, put a government with driving energy into power, rouse the world to a chorus of praise for our achievements? Suppose that the crusading courage of our young pilots, the vigilant energy of our soldiers and sailors, the brave uncomplaining endurance of our civilians, were harnessed to the imaginative construction of friendly international relationships based on mutual sacrifice and co-operative good will. Imagine what would happen if they were dedicated to revitalising the Church; rebuilding the slums; reinvigorating literature, music, and art; reorganising from top to bottom the economic system based on power and privilege; tackling the vexed problem of distribution; making equal education and opportunities available for all.

Would we not even in one decade be appreciably nearer to building Jerusalem in our green lanes and pleasant villages where now the incendiary bombs make hell upon earth, and the Nazi planes crash in an inferno of blazing oil and splintering steel? Can we lay the blame for Europe's catastrophe wholly upon others, when we have failed to lay even the foundation stones of our own City of God?

"Do I not have an account to settle between my soul and him?" wrote Dr. Harry Emerson Fosdick, the famous minister of Riverside Church in New York, as he apostrophised in penitence the American Unknown Soldier. "They sent men like me into the camps to awaken his idealism, to touch those secret holy springs within him so that with devotion, fidelity, loyalty, and self-sacrifice he might go out to war. . . . If wars were fought simply with evil things, like hate, it would be bad enough, but when one sees the deeds of war done with the loveliest faculties of the human spirit, he looks into the very pit of hell."

Have we not, too, an account to settle with the Unknown Pilot, whose ashes we take from his burnt-out aeroplane and cover with earth and grass? Is not the apathy or the misdirected energy of numerous guilty politicians responsible for the fires which consume those ardent young lives, and deprive them of the years of promise and achievement which should have been theirs? And are we not all responsible for choosing those guilty men, or for failing to remove them when they allowed our neighbours to become our enemies?

Even in these grievous days when the end of our night seems so far away, it is surely not too soon to vow that—by the sacrificial heroism of our youthful airmen, by the vigilant courage of our soldiers and sailors, by the bravery of our civilian defenders, and by the quiet endurance of British men and women who guard their homes and save their children while scorning to save themselves—we will never again ask a young generation to die for their country instead of using their superb qualities for the building of permanent peace.

23.   LONDON'S HOUR

IN THESE GRIMLY sunny days of mid-September, when I spend the entire morning getting three or four London telephone numbers from my flat and eventually make contact with Chelsea Town Hall, the conversation that ensues is invariably the same.

"No, madam. The delayed-action bomb behind your house has not yet exploded."

"In that case I suppose there's nothing to do but go on calling you up until it has."

"Well, madam, could you send instead of ringing? The telephone service is heavily engaged just now."

"How can I 'send'?" I inquire, remembering that several underground stations are now "out of action," and that a taxicab struggling to reach Chelsea from Portland Place may well have to make a detour all round Fulham and Hammersmith before it succeeds in finding an undamaged street leading down to the Embankment. "I'm all alone in a temporary flat at the other end of London."

"In that case I suppose you'll have to ring. But perhaps in a day or two you could come along . . ."

With my mind still on the unaccommodating bomb, I go into the nearest Post Office to assure Martin, in response to an agitated night letter telegram from New York, that I am alive up to date.

147

"Would you kindly give me a delayed-action cable form?" I say to the girl behind the counter, and cannot understand why she bursts out laughing.

A day or two later I do "come along" to Chelsea, not knowing whether I shall find my house still standing or, like so many others which once possessed the same qualities of history and grace, a sorry heap of ruins. To my surprise, the house appears unharmed and the barricades have been removed; the bomb has evidently exploded during the week-end in which the Town Hall was inaccessible to telephone calls. A temporary tidiness has been bestowed upon the forlorn Embankment by Chelsea's efficient A.R.P. service, but in the old familiar streets linking the King's Road with the river are hideous gaps and piles of debris which were once beautiful dwelling-houses. I have seen the names of some of their owners in the obituary column in *The Times* . . .

For once a raid-warning is not in operation, and I go inside my desolate house. During the days in which I was forbidden to enter, the clocks have all stopped ticking; a profound eerie silence greets me from the empty rooms which once echoed with the children's laughter, or heard the serial conversations between Martin and myself on the state of the world. All over the stairs, the bomb has shaken down dust and plaster; in the big sunny nursery where Richard and Hilary used to watch the barges chugging down the river, it lies thickly upon their little wooden tables and their small basket chairs. On the floor of my study at the top of the lofty house lie piles of books which Robert was about to clean with the vacuum when the time-bomb fell; amongst them the vacuum-cleaner has fallen drunkenly, a symbol of the innocent homely activities interrupted all over Europe by war.

"I can't bear this," I reflect miserably, as I pull down the few remaining pictures from the panelled walls of the long reverberating dining-room, and lay them face downwards on the dusty carpet. "I must store the furniture. We shan't be able to use the house again while the war lasts—not even if it goes on for years and years. Lilian can't be asked to come back with her baby to a bombarded London—and a six-storey house is too big and lonely just for Martin and me."

That evening a sympathetic letter arrives from a friend in New York.

"When you wrote me on August 30th," he comments, "you didn't know the half of it, as we say here."

I more than agree. Very soon I am to discover that I didn't know the half of it even when I read his letter. That night three hospitals and a number of churches are struck by bombs; thirty feet of a steeple in West London becomes a heap of rubble and debris. A famous hotel is hit, and a colonel and his wife who were sleeping in the damaged quarter are killed. Within a quarter-mile radius in Central London, every pane of glass in shops and houses is shattered. Fire breaks out at the bottom of one main thoroughfare, saving the Nazi airmen the trouble of dropping flares over our district. Fifty yards from my flat, two houses in an adjacent Crescent get direct hits and collapse with a roar; as I hear the bombs scream past our windows, the solid building above me cracks and shudders until I feel that the mass of steel and concrete is descending on my head. Sleepless after the tumult of the night, I go out at 7.30 a.m. into a calm sunny morning, and observe the smoke from an incendiary bomb which is still smouldering on the roof of the flats opposite our own.

That afternoon a friend and I attend, as visitors and observers, an emergency relief committee convened by the Society of Friends at an East End settlement close to the Bow Road, where a vigorous group of young men from a Quaker training centre in Birmingham has arrived to help in tackling the social problems created by the bombing of the crowded boroughs. As the usual route is now out of action, we make our way to the Bow Road by a compli-cated series of much-impeded conveyances.

"Thank God," I think, as we drive between its damaged houses, "that 'Uncle George' has passed beyond reach of the grief which the suffering of his old constituency would have caused him!"

Just as we arrive, the siren goes for the hundredth time, and our committee meeting is held in a whitewashed dug-out beneath the settlement, with a concrete ceiling and cushions on the floor.

Only a few days earlier, an aerial torpedo has fallen just outside the settlement, turning the surrounding region into a devastated area which I can now compare without reservation to the shattered towns that I saw in France at the end of the last war. It is hardly surprising that we share our business meeting with a number of mothers and small children who seek refuge in the friendly shelter. For some reason I am reminded of Swinburne's poem, "Watchman, what of the night?" If anything can give assurance that dawn will some day come, it is the tranquil determination of the Quaker leader, John Hoyland, and his group of young men, to do what they can towards clearing up the chaos brought to London's poorest dis-tricts by the generations of irresponsible politicians who never really believed that they who sow the wind must reap the whirlwind.

The committee is reluctantly obliged to conclude that the problem of the East End—its wrecked houses, its homeless families, its inadequate surface shelters which should have been deep and the increasingly grim conditions inside them—is one of such magnitude that only the government itself, or bodies such as the London County Council and the local authorities, possess sufficient resources to tackle it on a scale which can be effective. Already the raided populations, against the will of the government, have taken possession of the Underground Railways, which are excavated so far below the earth that no bomb can reach them. Night after night, men, women, and children equipped with rugs, mattresses, and cushions, queue up patiently at the gateways to these unofficial shelters which represent the only security that they, in their poverty and helplessness, have power to commandeer. It is beyond the scope of voluntary organisations to do more than ameliorate their needs, though they can usefully put pressure on lethargic authorities to take defence measures which should have been started months ago.

Feeling too weary to struggle again with the complications of shattered Tube and bus routes, my friends and I return by taxi to the comparative presentableness of Marylebone. Our journey back through the East End and the City resembles a nightmare fantasy by H. G. Wells. In the Mile End Road, every other house seems to have been demolished; again and again we encounter forlorn little processions of office workers, suitcases in hand, who have been driven from their homes or business premises by time-bombs. The narrow City streets involve a maze of temporary detours; craters in the roads are surrounded by uncleared heaps of bricks and stones; yawning gaps appear where banks and warehouses have stood. In the Euston Road we run into a traffic-block which crawls towards Marylebone. Eventually, in spite of the skeleton of Madame Tussaud's and the grim blackened façade of Chilton Court, we feel that we have returned to civilisation. Soon we are to learn that the remnants of civilisation are themselves only temporary.

Next morning my dentist insists upon removing a large double tooth from my long-suffering jaw. I almost welcome the operation, believing that it will provide a few moments of complete oblivion from the too-insistent present. But under the gas I go through a terrific bombardment, and come round just in time to hear the real siren wailing over the city.

When the raid is over and I have recovered from the anaesthetic, we go to inspect last night's damage. John Lewis's huge new store, we are told, is still burning from the bombs which set it alight while London was trying to sleep; Walpole's, and Bourne & Hollingsworth's, have both been gutted; Bond Street has almost as good a claim as Bow Road to be considered a devastated area. But the damage on Buckingham Palace, we hear, is already being repaired, and two days ago the one-ton time-bomb which threatened to destroy St. Paul's was removed and exploded in Hackney Marshes.

In Oxford Street the fire-hoses are still playing on John Lewis's ruined store. Whether they or the flames themselves have done more damage to its luxurious contents,

only the insurance companies can assess. Like the enormous skeleton of a prehistoric animal, the framework of
the great structure still stands, a doorless and windowless
erection of stone and steel. From the shattered window-
ledge of one upper storey, an orange silk vest flutters in
the breeze to remind passers-by of the elegant prosperity
which has already vanished.

Amongst the sight-seers watching the extinction of the
fire, I notice a veteran writer whom I have known at a
distance for many years: a novelist with a large public on
both sides of the Atlantic. Tall, gaunt, and utterly un-
moved, she gazes with pale sardonic eyes at the incredible
spectacle. She has refused, I learn later, to leave her West
End flat, though a time-bomb has fallen in the neighbourhood; she surmises, correctly, that when the bomb goes
off it will explode in the opposite direction. Unshaken and
intrepid, she insists upon remaining—Cassandra observing
the assault upon Troy.

That night, it is the turn of Regent Street to descend
from dignity and prosperity to the squalor of destruction
and dislocation. Walking to my flat as the quickest method
of returning from a visit to the Children's Overseas Reception Board, I find that hardly one Regent Street shop has
escaped with windows unsmashed or frontage unblack-
ened. At the top of the great curving road, Peter Robin-
son's dominant store surveys the scene of desolation with
a huge ugly gash in its side. The air is filled with the smell
of burning wood; the wide empty street lies ankle-deep in
glass. In one elegant furniture shop where the plate-glass
windows have been completely destroyed, two beautiful
yellow porcelain vases stand untouched on their pedestals.

Up and down the pavements walks a throng of spectators who utter hardly a word. If they are not the same

individuals who camped so placidly amid the trenches and barbed-wire entanglements in Hyde Park on August 4th, they are their nearest relatives; but now, like slumberers rudely awakened from sleep, they look shocked and blankly astonished. They pass indifferently beneath dangerous walls; showers of glass fall around them as they move. A stalwart steel-helmeted policeman remonstrates with weary resignation: "Naw, then, show a little common sense, cawn't yer!"

This, I remind myself again, is war—war as Madrid, Pekin, and Helsinki have known it. I don't think I ever quite believed that it would come to London; but now, after other parts of Britain have suffered, the wheel of fate has revolved to bring London her hour.

The eyes of the world are turned upon her as she nerves herself to face her long ordeal.

24. UNIVERSITY METROPOLIS

NOT EVEN THE MOST biassed apologist for the British railways in wartime could insist that the train from Paddington to Oxford is making rapid progress. There have been air-raid alarms in both London and Reading on this morning of late September, and the loss of time on train journeys to the west gradually extends from half-an-hour to two hours and more. Even on this wide main line, so much more fortunate than most, which has no tunnels to tumble upon its steel rails nor bridges to collapse under them, "mishaps" occur which involve long detours round unexpected stations, and City workers struggling to reach their offices from the Home Counties or the outer suburbs are constantly greeted by the dreaded injunction: "All change!"

At Reading the train arrives late, and waits for a very long time. Crowding the station from end to end are troops with their kit and evacuated civilians with their baggage, dejectedly waiting to go to Oxford, Bristol, Gloucester, or South Wales. The platform is piled with huge bags of undelivered mail, and littered with fragments of torn paper and straw. Shabby East End women with small children standing forlornly among the mailbags have grey faces and deep circles beneath their eyes, as though they have not slept for weeks . . .

Our long delay is suddenly interrupted by a train filled with evacuee children from London, which actually runs rapidly through the station towards some nominally "safe area" in Wales or Cornwall. The small boys and girls at the windows cheer and wave their hands, and the mothers and children waiting on the platform wave back. The departure of these families from London has been no panic evacuation, but an orderly and often too prolonged exodus arranged according to an emergency time-table. Their patient air of resignation recalls, not the wild flight from Paris in June, but the grim stoicism of the Spanish Civil War. I remember the comment that I made to Martin at Southampton on September 2, 1939, and whisper to myself: "Madrid!"

When the train starts again and I eventually arrive at Oxford for two days' exploration of my old University, where I spent the first year of one war and now wish to examine the effects of another, it is already 1.30 P.M. As we run in slowly past the cemetery and the gas-works, which blot out the grey familiar spires, a dozen circling aeroplanes roar overhead. They are perpetually on guard above this city in the Thames valley, where the long history of our island culture is not merely recorded, but irreplaceably embodied in the vulnerable glory of glass and the inimitable curves of ancient stone. All through the hours that I spend amongst the lovely remembered shrines of a sorrowful youth no more tragic than this present, the autumn air echoes with the sound of whirring engines and rushing wings, which at intervals become swiftly visible beneath the azure afternoon sky or the sanguine pageant of sunset cloud.

At the station I fight my way through a noisy pandemonium of bicycles, perambulators, trolleys, trunks, troops, students, mothers, and children, and after much strenuous persuasion induce a tired waitress in a dark, overcrowded café in Cornmarket Street to serve me with a belated luncheon. As I walk up St. Giles towards Somerville, my old college where I have arranged to stay, I find myself again facing the tall slender war memorial, like a graceful lily on a long pale stalk. Its short inscription still wistfully commemorates "those who fought and those who fell," twenty-five years ago.

The quiet of Somerville is almost audible after the clamour in the crowded town. A dignified entrance, beautifully planned in modern fashion to emphasize the deep arch above the college garden, has replaced the ancient cottages of my student days. Complete silence envelops the wide green lawns, now made almost a quadrangle by the encircling grace of recent buildings. There is no one about to tell me where my room is, or whether I am really expected. I wander slowly down the central path towards the West Building, where Winifred Holtby's ghost still walks for me among the drooping sycamores outside the room where we crouched on the rug before her fire when the wind moaned on winter evenings. There are no students now in these rooms, I am soon to learn; they have been taken over for the duration of the war by the young nurses from the Radcliffe Infirmary next door.

I am moving back under the archway in search of a stray scout who will direct me to my room, when a door suddenly swings open and the Dean of the College appears, carrying a basket of autumn berries and Michaelmas daisies. To me she still looks identical with the juvenile don of two decades ago, but our conversation could only have occurred in 1940.

"You'll hardly find us 'as usual,' " she tells me. "We've

had half London turned into the city—and a large part of Kent as well."

"Where do most of them go?"

"Oh, all over the place; I can't think why we haven't had them here. The men's colleges have been full of them —not even excluding Christ Church. They've had babies' nappies drying in Tom Quad for the first time all through its history."

"You've had no bombs here yet, then?" I inquire, as yet unaware that my now perpetual companion, the air-raid siren, will follow me to Oxford this very evening, sounding its warning just after a stick of bombs has been flung down promiscuously upon the rural heights of Boar's Hill five miles away.

"Not so far," answers the Dean. "The nearest was at Ferry Hinksey, and that was only a little one."

"It seems odd that you don't get them in a place as congested as this—to say nothing of the motor works. Do you think it's fear of reprisals on Heidelberg?"

"Well, they say here that Hitler's keeping Oxford for himself. He wants it to look as it always has when he comes to get his Honorary Degree!"

I discover my room, leave my bag, and go out for a solitary walk round the city. The creepers are turning red on the walls of Balliol College, as they were in 1914 when I first came to Oxford, and again in 1919 when I returned there, still so young in years, after a lifetime of war— never dreaming that it could come again, in a yet crueller fashion, long before I was old. In St. John's College the cloisters are now strutted with timber, but the famous garden, with its lawns of golden-green velvet and its massed borders of fuchsias and asters, shows no symptom of war.

Passing by the iron gates of Trinity, which is strangely combining the instruction of the Officers' Training Corps with a clergymen's conference, I find Blackwell's bookshop still wearing the serene, untroubled face which it managed to preserve throughout World War No. 1. With academic impartiality, its furthest window displays, side by side, "Christian Pacifism Re-examined," by Cecil John Cadoux, and Leonard Woolf's latest publication, "The War for Peace." Even the incongruously modern extension of the Bodleian Library at the Holywell end of Broad Street has somehow failed to overshadow the ancient imperturbableness of Blackwell's. A strong smell of ether unexpectedly emanates from the new chrome-yellow building; it is explained by the temporary presence of "The Emergency Blood Transfusion Service," which announces itself, in large and appropriately scarlet letters, as functioning within.

New College, which was my husband's and should have been my brother's, I discover to be still behaving as a college, where undergraduates are expected in a fortnight for the Michaelmas Term. Later, I shall learn from one of its dons, who was Martin's contemporary, that the work of the University is less interrupted by this war than by the last, which practically emptied it of men. When the colleges open two weeks hence, about half the normal contingent of students will come up. The military age for undergraduates is now twenty, which enables them to do two years at Oxford and take certificates that after the war will probably entitle them to a Degree.

Even to-day, when most of the students have not yet appeared, there seems no lack of men in the city streets. Beyond Magdalen Bridge there are many more—men of a different type doing work of a different kind. For the great motor industry begun by Lord Nuffield when he was a garage proprietor at Cowley named William Morris, lies beyond Magdalen Bridge, and the population of Oxford on the Cowley side of the river is now greater than the population in the University half of the city.

The lawn of New College, sloping downwards at the edges like a gigantic pie-dish, has the same fabric-like smoothness as the lawns of St. John's. Its pink rosebushes, standing placidly in their damp fragrant beds, display an air of reassuring perpetuity, and the window-sills of the college rooms are vivid with scarlet geraniums. The ancient ivied walls, unlike many old walls in London, still stand undamaged beyond the trees which have survived so much history. I glance at the Cloisters but do not enter, for too fierce a nostalgia threatens my powers of endurance. Within these Cloisters, sixteen years ago, Martin put my engagement ring on my finger, and speculated: "I wonder if the next generation will ever come here?"

I doubt now whether the next generation will, even if there should still be a college to come to. Richard is in America, and the times are out of joint.

From New College, as the guide books say, it is only a step to the doors of All Souls. I go there to renew my recollection of its twin white binoculars, and stand outside a locked gate inexorably labelled: "This College is closed to visitors until further notice." I remember doing Pass Moderations there in June 1915, and the difficulty of giving my mind to Plato's "Apology" and the intricacies of Greek Unseen Proses when so many beloved friends were serving at the front. . . . It was, in fact, almost as hard to pass an examination in 1915, as it is to write a book in 1940. . . .

I had thought Oxford station as closely crammed with

humanity as any limited space could possibly achieve; but now, looking at the High Street, I find that I was wrong. Up and down the great curving thoroughfare, packed almost too close for movement and pushing one another from the pavement into the gutter, struggles a crowd which varies from harassed dons in tweeds to weary homeless mothers from Poplar or Plaistow dragging small bewildered children by the hand. Carfax, I perceive, looking up the road to the clock-tower above the crossroads which divide Cornmarket Street from St. Aldate's, resembles nothing so much as Charing Cross in the pre-war rush-hour.

To escape from the pressure of the drifting, motiveless human multitude, I turn into the gateway of University College. The chapel windows, I notice, are boarded up; the Shelley Memorial has been removed to some stronghold beyond the reach of bombs. I approach the friendly college porter with the now customary question, for the porch is littered with suitcases, hold-alls, umbrellas, and gas-masks which do not suggest the presence of the normal inhabitants.

"What's happening here? Is this college still a college?"

"Well," he answers, "we're opening again in two weeks' time, but we aren't exactly a college at the moment. We're full up with evacuees."

"You mean from the East End?"

"No, they're not East Enders, ours are not—though there's plenty of them in the town. We've got a lot of evacuees from Ashford, Kent. There was five thousand of 'em came to Oxford. We've got fifteen thousand extra people in the city altogether, pushed in here from other places."

"But you won't be able to keep them when the undergraduates come?"

"Oh, no. The authorities are gradually finding 'em
billets. They came here first because they'd nowhere to go,
and Jerry was bombin' them every night. We've been a
sort of clearing house, as you might say."

That evening I am to learn from the Somerville Bursar
that there is not a room to be rented in Oxford, nor a bed
to be hired in a local hotel. Even at Somerville many
students will have to sleep out when the term begins, in
order that the nurses from the Infirmary may remain in
the West Building. The college, the Bursar tells me, is
putting up evacuee strangers of every kind. Many have no
better claim to stay there than the fact that they had a
niece or a godchild at Somerville long ago. No wonder,
I reflect, struggling up the High, that the shops are as
crowded with buyers as the stores at sale-time in a capital
city, and the streets so jammed with traffic that it is impossible to cross them except at marked corners. The
perpetual din, combined with the incessant zoom of the
circling aeroplanes, leaves me deaf for several seconds
when I emerge from it once more into the comparative
quiet of St. Giles's.

Why, I wonder, as I return slowly to Somerville, do I
still feel like a student here, though I am a married woman
in my forties with two children reaching adolescence?
Whence comes this same awe at the dignity of the college,
this same feeling of shy timidity in the presence of senior
Somerville dons? Is it because this city—where even the
Examination Schools have been transformed into a hospital as they were twenty-five years ago—resembles the
city of my student days so much more closely than at any
time in the two decades between? What has become of

those intervening years—the years which for me will be for ever identified with Winifred Holtby's life and work?

They are gone, just as surely as she is gone; they have vanished with their confident young dreams of a new society built upon the ruins of the Victorian age which the First World War demolished, and their vision of a unified international community with its centre at Geneva and its instrument the League of Nations. I know now that the hopes of those years will never return in my lifetime. The world of men, and especially the world of statesmen, loves the pursuit of power by the old destructive methods far too well to be readily dissuaded from it by a few idealists with disconcerting, incongruous dreams of a City of God. . . .

When this war came, I remember, I regretted in moments of weakness that my children had ever been born. Now I know that they are my only guarantee for the survival of that vision which still summons me from comfort and compromise to obey, without hope of success, the once optimistic challenge of my youth. For though I must die, youth itself is immortal; its star begins to ascend the heaven of the future as mine sinks below the brief zenith of my generation. Some day, accepted as its own by a New World and a wiser civilisation, Richard and Hilary may live to realise our vanished hopes and fulfil our lost ideals.

25. EVACUEE DEPOT

"TALKING ABOUT THE EAST END," says the Somerville Dean after dinner, "did you get as far as the Majestic Cinema in the Botley Road?"

"No," I reply. "What with one college being a government department, and another an evacuee depot, and a third continuing as a college, I found my time was filled up just by going round the town."

"Well, if you want to see *the* evacuee depot, you'd better visit the Majestic to-morrow. At the moment it's our Problem. You'll find the local paper full of letters about it."

Next morning, half a mile beyond the station, I reach a Railway Mission Church in the Botley Road. A printed poster outside the church offers a sound piece of advice: "If your knees knock, kneel on them." How usefully I might have followed it on numerous occasions in London, I am thinking, when three stout women wearing fur coats over cotton frocks pass the church and me without apparently noticing either. Feeling certain that they are amongst the cinema's temporary inhabitants, I walk on in the direction whence they have come.

In a few moments I reach the Majestic, which stands back from the road behind a plot of communal grass. The advertisement of the last picture show has not yet been removed; appropriately enough it was "Babes in Arms," featuring Mickey Rooney. Amongst the rugs and per-ambulators on the short dry grass lie pieces of chewed apple-core, fragments of orange peel, and the inevitable sheets of torn dirty newspaper which indicate, like a paper trail, the presence of an evacuee population the moment that it moves from its normal environment.

As I enter the cinema, a familiar and overpowering stench strikes me in the face like a blow. Where did I last encounter it, I wonder, and then I remember; it was the smell of the crowded ladies' saloon on the night boat during a rough Channel crossing. Gradually my nose becomes accustomed to it as my eyes also accommodate themselves to the unillumined twilight inside the building. Covering the floor beneath the upturned velveteen seats of the cinema chairs, disorderly piles of mattresses, pillows, rugs, and cushions indicate the "pitches" staked out by the different evacuated families. Many of the women, too dispirited to move, still lie wearily on the floor with their children beside them in the fetid air, though the hour is eleven A.M. and a warm sun is shining cheerfully on the city streets. Between the mattresses and cushions, the customary collection of soiled newspapers and ancient apple-cores is contributing noticeably to the odoriferous atmosphere. A few small boys, evidently set to the task by the organisers on the floor above, are making a determined attack on the extensive squalor with besoms and brooms.

At the end of one row of cinema seats sits a small stout woman of indeterminate age, dressed in a loose-fitting dark skirt and a blouse which has long ceased to be any particular colour. She has the same sallow skin, and the same heavy rings round her eyes, as I noticed amongst the evacuated mothers on Reading station.

"How long have you been here?" I ask her.

"It's three weeks come to-morrow," she tells me. "I come 'ere from Poplar."

"Did you choose Oxford, or were you sent here?"

"Well, you see, miss, it's like this. After me house was bombed, me and the kid was in the schoolhouse, and I says to Miss Rackham—that's the schoolmistress—I says, 'I've got four children evacuated to Cowley'—well looked after, they are, too, miss—'and if there's any choice it's Oxford for me.' So she fixes it for me some'ow, and I come down 'ere in the coach."

"Was your house completely destroyed, then?"

"Pretty near. Me oldest boy was 'ome on leave at the time, and what with the water main being bombed and the gas cut off, I couldn't even make 'im a cup of tea. After three days 'e got fed up with it and no wonder, what with the door bein' 'arf off and no glass in the windows. 'E says, 'Look 'ere, Mum, I'm off to Oxford to see the kids,' and I says, 'I don't blame you, lad! You go, and I'll follow you if I can.'"

"So now you've got your whole family down here?"

"Aye—all but me 'usband. He's been missin' for five weeks. I've tried to inquire, but there's so many others. There was nine hundred of them copped it at one time...."

It seems a situation for which no real comfort exists....

"At least you've got your children safe," I say lamely.

"Yes—that's true; and it wouldn't be too bad if it weren't for the food."

"The food?" I inquire. It seems a sudden transition from the tragedy of her lost husband.

"Aye, the food. Tea's just like dish-water, and the meat they give you leaves you famished all day."

I make a mental resolution to inspect the commissariat department before I leave the building.

"And what about the children?" I continue, looking at the little flaxen-haired girl lying back in a mail-cart and sucking half an orange which will soon be due for disposal in the usual manner by throwing it on the floor.

"Well, all she gets is just a bit of what you have your-self, and that's no food for a child."

"How old is she?"

"Just eighteen months. She's my youngest."

"Don't they give her any milk, then?"

"Oh, *milk!* Yes, she gets plenty of that."

After learning from the disgruntled mother that lava-tory accommodation is provided on a sufficient scale for everyone who wishes to have a daily wash, I go across the passage to the canteen where meals are served. Here a series of exhortations pinned up on the walls show the determined though Sisyphus-like attacks which the har-assed local authorities are making on potential disease and primitive standards of cleanliness.

"Mothers possessing babies' feeding bottles with teats," I read, "*must* produce them at 10 A.M. every morning so that they can be boiled."

On the opposite wall, two "Important Notices" indicate that comfort and advice are readily available to stranded maternity.

"Expectant Mothers.—Please report to Sister in Charge if they feel at all unwell."

"Nursing Mothers who would like to consult the Sister in Charge on dieting problems will be very welcome."

A familiar verse from the Gospels comes suddenly into my head: "Woe unto them that are with child, and to them that give suck, in those days . . ." Intolerably oppressed by the blind cruelty of war, I move to the end of the long room to read the most conspicuous injunction of all:

WILL ALL EVACUEES
PLEASE
DO THEIR VERY BEST TO CO-OPERATE
WITH THE STAFF TO KEEP THE
BUILDING CLEAN AND TIDY.

Upstairs in the administrative offices where doctors, nurses, organisers, and canteen workers are all to be found, I learn that the authority responsible for the management of the cinema is the Public Assistance Department of the Oxford City Council. The nurses available for help and consultation belong to the staff of the Medical Officer of Health. I go into the kitchen, and find two members of the Women's Voluntary Services in charge. One was at Winifred Holtby's school in Scarborough; the other is a trained cook and domestic expert whose husband is an officer on service in West Africa. They are slicing large slabs of jellied galantine which smell very appetising; several dozen must be cut up to provide lunch for a thousand evacuees, and I offer to assist in this useful if greasy occupation. As I slice with considerably less dexterity than the practised voluntary staff, I learn that the depot is designed to provide for an average of seven hundred refugees. This number, they tell me, will be constantly maintained; as soon as private billets are found for each family, others will be brought in from the devastated East End.

"They're all the same," one of the W.V.S. organisers tells me. "When they first come, they're so dazed and quiet after all they've been through, that they're grateful for anything. Then, gradually, they begin to find fault with things, especially the food. When they really get grousing, you know they're back to normal!"

"One woman downstairs told me the tea was dishwash," I say in corroboration. "I expect she's used to what we called 'sergeant-major's tea' in the last war. 'Hot as hell, sweet as love, black as death'—as a restaurant I know in New York describes its coffee."

"Well, you shall have a cup, and see what it's like for yourself. We'll all have one."

While the kettle is boiling, she shows me the large extra stoves put up by the City engineers in a kitchen designed to serve one hundred and thirty—patrons of the cinema and the adjacent ice rink who came in for occasional meals. I see the big vats of boiling potatoes and greens, and a large cupboard filled with fresh apples and pears contributed by local owners of gardens.

"It's all getting organised now, and we've got plenty of helpers," my informant explains. "It was the first few days, when the refugees simply turned up before anything was ready for them, that nearly finished me off."

I thank her, drink the excellent cup of tea prepared, finish slicing my slab of galantine, wash the grease from my fingers and depart. Efficiency, I reflect as I walk through Walton Street back to Somerville, is certainly bringing gradual order out of squalor and chaos, while the food and health of the evacuees are under competent if frequently defeated control. What remains to be done is harder and cannot be achieved in a day, nor a month, nor a year; it is nothing less than the elimination of those too long tolerated differences of standards which evacuation schemes have revealed throughout the country. The apple-cores and the soiled newspapers will not disappear until the West End really knows and cares how the East End lives.

26. INDUSTRIAL MIDLANDS

"No," REPEATS the Euston inquiry official firmly. "We cannot guarantee you a connection to-morrow. Nothing doing on this line at the moment. If you take my advice, you'll go by Birmingham."

So the long trek across the Midlands begins. Soon after nine on a morning of early October, I catch a bus from the Berkshire village where I have spent the week-end. At Reading, that still harassed and even more crowded junction, the train is already twenty minutes late. Gradually losing more, it arrives at Oxford by the time that it should have been reaching Birmingham. We crawl past Leamington and Warwick, and gradually approach the Black Country, flat, grey, smoke-ridden, in which all the gloom and depression of wartime seems to be embodied.

The one inconspicuous feature of the landscape is damage from bombs, though I have been told repeatedly in London that air-raids have severely punished these Midland areas. Even near the railway line, where attacks might well be expected, there is little trace of devastation. One large crater in country fields, one section of smashed

Note: The intensive air-attacks on Midland towns which began with the Coventry raid on November 14th-15th started four days after this book had gone to the printers. They were at least as destructive as any London raid, and considerably altered the proportion of damage experienced by the industrial Midlands.

goods-yards near a busy railway station, complete the story of visible havoc. Later, in a Staffordshire village, my hostess confirms these transient observations from her own experience.

"I saved up petrol and went to see Kathleen," she tells me of her daughter at Cheltenham. "It was a hundred-mile drive right through the middle of the country, and I didn't see a wrecked house or a bomb crater the whole way there."

Except for an exemplary increase in cabbages, the greener parts of Staffordshire look just as I have always known them. It is not the tranquil spreading fields but the trains which run through them that are different. The slowness and infrequency of these local trains cause them to be crowded to a degree which recalls unflattering stories of Moscow. From end to end civilian travellers stand among their suitcases in the corridor, and every type of railway carriage—not excluding the goods van—is crammed with soldiers and their bulky equipment. Invasion has still not come, and all the fighting is in the air; yet the three million troops in the country appear to be perpetually on the move. The weary civilian wonders why. Can it be to provide them with a semblance of occupation? Most of the young men convey the impression that a few days' hard work would do them no harm.

After nine hours' lethargic and comfortless travel by a circuitous route, I reach Stoke-on-Trent. In London rumour has insisted that the station has been "demolished," but except for the sensible removal of the glass from the platform roof, I perceive no change. After the crucifixion of London and the transformation of my old University to a sad and shabby metropolis, the normality of my native Potteries brings a comforting reassurance. Taking another local train, I finally arrive at a village ten miles from Stoke on the edge of the moorlands where Stafford-shire and Derbyshire meet. The tenuous mists of twilight are rising from the steep grey-green fields as I walk uphill with my host through the warm damp lane which leads from the little station in the valley to his house on the heights.

When supper is over and we sit before a comfortable fire, my hostess shows me photographs of her two tall sons who have just returned to Oundle, and her daughter whose school, in the centre of England, is disturbed neither by sirens nor by bombs. After living, with few and short intervals, the life of a war-obsessed Londoner for more than a year, I am enviously astonished to find that in some country districts the war has exacted no sacri-fice and has left unchanged the placid regularity of peace-time. This second war, like the last, has wrecked—for how long?—my personal life; it has taken my children away from me, sent my husband after them to America, compelled me, like so many London dwellers, to abandon my home; yet here is a family for whom war has not even affected the daily household routine.

Yet even here the sense of escape is not quite complete; if plague, pestilence, or famine should come, these hills and moors can raise no ramparts against them. Already, now that darkness shrouds the surrounding fields, we hear from afar the hesitant bumping of German bombers look-ing for Liverpool or Crewe, and the sawing moan of pri-vate sirens from the small local factories which have industrialised the valleys of this prosperous countryside. But the visitation of real war as we know it in the South seems remote and improbable. That night I sleep in a fashion long forgotten by Londoners who live in the noisy centre of the city, or spend their nights in the menacing, explosion-ridden darkness of country districts in the Home Counties.

Early next morning, my host takes me to see a valley factory. No bombs have yet dropped near it, but it receives private alarm signals from several surrounding towns, and the inescapable Nazi bombers fly by night over its protecting hills. Is there any place now on this small island where that heavy uneven throb, as though the bomber were climbing a steep mountain, has never been heard?

At the factory an escorting warden shows me with pride their up-to-date A.R.P. equipment—the fire-fighting apparatus, the protective uniforms, the sandbagged shelters and posts. I am invited to climb halfway up the iron ladder leading to the lofty green-painted tank where the factory "roof-spotter" watches for approaching bombers; I learn that a new building being erected for "government work" must have a tin roof because of the mysterious shortage of cement. All over this Midland country there must be hundreds of small businesses to which war has temporarily brought more prosperity than adversity, and which can therefore afford to spend hundreds of pounds upon precautions against bombers who may produce a real threat once throughout its duration.

From the factory I am driven into the Potteries, that familiar district of slag-heaps and tall smoking chimneys where at last I am shown a few places in which bombs have fallen. But these sporadic acres of devastation are difficult to distinguish from the débris normally caused in this district by "wear and tear." So much of the Potteries has reached a stage of dilapidation which nothing but complete clearance of the particular area could cure, that more than once my commiseration is misplaced.

"You've had some trouble here!" I remark, with sympathetic recollection of World's End, Chelsea, or the Mile End Road, and am cheerfully corrected by my escorts: "Oh, no! That wasn't done by bombs. It was like that long before the war!"

At my birthplace, Newcastle-under-Lyme, I spend half-an-hour with a public official who gives me the latest news of the borough. Its pleasant residential streets suggest that neither wars nor rumours of wars have ever disturbed it, but I am assured that—though there was only one casualty—a total of one hundred and seventy-five bombs has been dropped on Newcastle alone.

"How did the A.R.P. services function?" I inquire as usual, and am rewarded with more than customary frankness.

"Those bombs did the trick. Until they fell, every war organisation in the place wanted to be top dog, and local government wasn't so much a matter of war as diplomacy. The moment there was some real work to do, the squabbles stopped overnight."

I learn with regret that Newcastle's first-class scheme for slum clearance and town-planning—one of the most enlightened and imaginative in this country—has now been indefinitely postponed in favour of "war effort." Though Newcastle Corporation had bought up land for miles round the borough, the rehousing of an area which urgently requires the relief of overcrowding is ended for the duration. The necessary materials are not available to builders, and building societies will no longer lend. Newcastle is now the only borough which flies the Union Jack permanently over its Guildhall; its Councillors have exchanged the constructive schemes of peace for the remedial auxiliary services of war.

Later in the morning, I talk to a young electrician who specialises in the care of electrical installations in biscuit and tile factories. His occupation, he tells me, has not been greatly affected by the war. The roofing-tile manufacturers have had to close owing to the arrest of building, but the glazed-tile manufacturers just manage to keep open owing to demands from North and South America, and some of the local biscuit manufacturers are "helping out" former London competitors whose factories have been bombed.

"This war has livened up the export of biscuits, because markets abroad have had to be found," the young man explains. "These firms get quite a number of orders now from South America and the Dominions."

"But suppose really severe bombing should start here as it has in London? Would these small trades be able to carry on?"

"Well, so far it doesn't seem as if we get bombed except when lights are actually showing. You see, this is a very difficult area for a bomber to find any worth-while objective. It isn't one large industrial city; it's a series of small towns and villages with fields in between. And then everything in the valley is always covered by a pall of smoke. The manufacturers who tried to contribute to smoke-abatement schemes now get encouraged to make as much smoke as possible."

So this accounts for the whole district looking even dirtier than usual, I reflect, as the electrician goes on to explain that even continuous bombing could not affect the Potteries as it has affected London.

"There's as big a volume of industrial production going

on here as anywhere, but it would be very difficult to stop because the whole district is an area of small businesses. If you knocked out a dozen, it wouldn't make much difference to the total output. Then, as you know, it's a tradition here for the workers to live near their work. You can't stop production by dislocating transport when everyone can get to business on his feet."

I have been told that the young man is a keen trade unionist, so I ask him as I leave how the war has affected the movement in the Potteries which first began to acquire strength at the end of the last war. He tells me eagerly that trade unionism, especially in Hanley, has been strengthened by the bringing in of "foreigners" from London, Liverpool, or Birmingham, who come from districts where the movement is strong.

"There's a typical saying in the Potteries, 'If you do owt for nowt, do it for yoursen.' It's this kind of attitude that must be broken down before our unions can hope to get strong."

After a convivial luncheon at the Grand Hotel in Hanley, where the food seems as little affected by the war as everything else in this area, I call on the Editor of the Staffordshire *Evening Sentinel.* I have several questions to put to him about the production of local newspapers in wartime, but I soon discover that, like the experienced newspaperman whom I know him to be, he is interviewing me rather than I him. In common with most intelligent editors, he is critical of national censorship methods —an attitude which he expresses in his newspaper on the Saturday after my visit when reporting the bombing of a London public school:

"Obviously, air raid anonymity is essential in some circumstances, because the enemy does not always know where he has been; but in this case, either it was necessary to disguise the location altogether, or the name of the school could be given right out.

"The censorship should have regard to the acute anxiety, or even distress, which may be caused by partial or vague news. Better no news than that."

To-day, over tea and toast in his comfortable office, he wants to check the official reports on London air-raid damage by my personal statements. Do I know, he adds, whether any big London gasometer has been hit? He has a theory that these huge circular cisterns will not explode, but will burn like a candle, and he is anxious to test it. I cannot, however, tell him of one gasometer that has actually been bombed, though I know from my own experience of several fractured gas mains. For long enough now it has been impossible to get any toast at my flat, and even the boiling of a kettle is a dilatory affair.

I am finally rewarded by inspecting for myself the wartime manufacture of a newspaper. It is typical of Staffordshire that the whole paper should be produced in one building, and the printing room is only a short walk from the editorial office. Here I start one of the printing presses myself—a light task fulfilled by touching a button —and learn that machinery had just been installed for producing a twenty-four-page newspaper when the size of the *Sentinel* was reduced to six pages by paper restrictions.

At a public tea where my host and I have an appointment with the local organiser of Women's Voluntary Services, who is taking me to inspect her first-aid post, I meet a number of leading Staffordshire women who include an ex-Member of Parliament. By their generously expressed admiration for the behaviour of Londoners, they fill me with a sense of unworthiness. They hope, most anxiously, that I have not been discouraged by my own experiences; and I think guiltily of the terror that I still suffer when I recall a Kensington house swaying in the track of a bomb like a ship at sea, and the melancholy that overcomes me when I picture Richard's painting-table and Hilary's discarded high chair covered with plaster and dust . . .

The first-aid post, I find, has been established, characteristically enough, in a disused pottery. The old building has already been partly destroyed by a pre-war fire, and looks as though it had been thoroughly "plastered" by an unusually effective air-raid. In one part of the burned-out yard which is now used as a car-park, a surviving mosaic paving-stone, dated 1750, indicates that the pottery once belonged to the Copeland family. The local A.R.P., W.V.S., and First Aid services have shown great ingenuity in converting this ruin into a rest-room, canteen, and consulting room; but after witnessing so many air-raids I cannot help wondering what the effect of a real bombing attack would be upon this derelict expanse.

On the whole, I conclude, as I retire to bed after the exacting day, the Potteries are quite enjoying the war. For an industrial area, the six towns which Arnold Bennett described as five contain a minimum of shattered homes and broken hearts. Here the air warfare which has brought horror and grief to London has come near enough to stimulate and unite, but not so near as to destroy and depress. It is the first district of its kind that I have encountered, and I envy ruefully the wisdom of my ancestors who conducted their births, marriages, and deaths within twenty miles of Stoke-on-Trent.

Next day—since I am not immediately returning to London—I endure another long cross-country journey, involving four changes with an hour's wait at each. The second of the five trains by which I travel has actually a restaurant car, and I listen over luncheon to a mercantile marine officer, fortified by half a bottle of Grave, describing the evacuation of Dunkirk to his Territorial companion.

"Anything that floated was there—any old thing from private yachts to battleships. When Harland & Woolf's engineers found men were wanted, they volunteered to a man and paid their own charabanc down to Dover. . . . Yes, I went along with a tug—half tight all the time. Bought a bottle of whisky for each trip. . . . Didn't care a damn in the end whether I got bombed or not. . . ."

In spite of the good lunch with its lurid narrative accompaniment, the later stages of my weary southward journey suggest to me that what, for the past few days, I have been witnessing is not merely a country at war, but the closing stages of a civilisation. It was not an equally distributed civilisation; my two hours in the Oxford cinema re-emphasised the shameful standards of living which we and our rulers have shut away in the East Ends of overcrowded cities and complacently forgotten. But it was a civilisation which had its points. Following the energetic lead of the United States, it was in process of mastering discomfort and eliminating the avoidable waste of time and energy. Its chief god was the god of speed, and despite the terrifying rapidity of modern war machines, that god was not wholly malevolent.

I believed the invention of the aeroplane to be the greatest evil which man had inflicted on himself until, a year or so before this war, I read in the newspapers of a baby girl with an open safety-pin in her throat conveyed by air from Guernsey to the Children's Hospital at Great Ormond Street in time for the specialists there to save her life. To-day Guernsey is in the hands of the Nazis, and Great Ormond Street has been repeatedly bombed. Was the baby snatched by its skilled surgeons from certain death only to fall victim to the Nazi invaders?

"We follow," wrote Tom Paine, "with a sense of shame and horror man's advance through the middle and higher barbarism, looking back almost with regret to the period of savagery when human progress exhibited a comparatively beneficent aspect." In the civilisation which our "higher barbarism" produced there was much to be justly admired, but now it has gone, sacrificed to its suicidal "impulse of death." Comfort and speed were its main objectives, and to-day, in this island, both are vanishing. That civilisation is unlikely to return, for those who made it have killed it themselves.

Some day this England, or what is left of it, will have to build another—founded upon a more spiritual and therefore a more enduring basis. In spite of bombs, submarines, epidemics and starvation, some of us will survive to assist in that reconstruction. We shall deserve to take part only if we endeavour to make the new civilisation—like "progress" in the "savage" eras which preceded ours—wear a more "beneficent aspect" than the epoch in which our efforts to ameliorate the society of our time have come to an end.

27. LIVING DANGEROUSLY

WE STAND OPPOSITE a great newspaper house on a mid-October morning after picking our way gingerly to the pavement through fragments of stone and typed sections of newssheets flung by the explosion across the crowded thoroughfare.

By this time the damage of public buildings has almost ceased to attract attention, but the fame of this particular institution gives news value to the assault. Its method of recording current history, judiciously fused with a note of excitement whenever the story of some conspicuous British exploit confronts the narrator, has become as familiar to us as our grandmother scolding the milkman down the telephone or the nightly protests of the latest baby.

Last night, several residents excitedly assert, they heard the bomb drop when the raid was at its height. Unlike most bombs, my neighbours explain, it fell three floors before it exploded and left in the dignified façade of the great modern structure a jagged central hole which suggests the nocturnal activities of gigantic rodents.

A Cockney girl in the little crowd echoed my thoughts.

"Ow! Don't it look as if the mice 'ad been at it!"

So they've got their objective at last, I reflect, remembering nights when bombs intended for this famous building screamed past the windows of our block of flats and fell like infernal hail all over our district. There was the September evening when X. Avenue was hit; the October midnight when a delayed-action bomb dropped in Z. Street with a strange unexplosive thud like a huge rock flung from the top of a mountain. . . . Hearing voices and feet above my basement refuge, and recalling nights when the occupants of neighbouring flats were hastily evacuated into ours owing to the presence of time-bombs, I wondered uneasily whether I ought to collect my usual paraphernalia—mattress, eiderdown, handbag, and gas-mask—and sally forth with them into the street. . . .

To-day I have received, with unusual rapidity, an air-mail letter from my New York friend who fought with an American Division in France in 1918. Living in London, he writes, must be very much the same as living at the front in the previous war—only now it is worse.

"You are not under constant artillery fire—you had to be pretty close to a whizz-bang to have it get you—you are under constant bombing, much more terrific, much more devastating, and capable of reaching much further. If one can put one's morals and one's philosophy of creative life behind one, it must be damned exciting . . ."

Evidently, I conclude, as I turn homewards from the scattered untidiness of papers and bricks, he has forgotten how excessively boring danger becomes when you are in it perpetually; how completely it destroys concentration upon ideas, books, music, philosophy, and other things far more interesting than the mere preservation of life.

Those first days of the London Blitzkrieg have gone with their moments in which, had it not been for thoughts of Martin and the children, I should almost have enjoyed the peculiar zest of dodging death. The zest has vanished, but the aching, haunting memory of Richard and Hilary remains.

"My darlings, shall I ever see you again?" I speculate for the hundredth time as I walk past the blackened, still smouldering walls of Maple's store at the corner of Tottenham Court Road. "I couldn't wish to have you here now in the midst of this battered England—though for all their boredom and grimness, I wouldn't for anything have missed the past two months myself. . . . But your very existence weakens me; it turns me into a coward, a seeker of security; it entangles me in troublesome moral questions—common to how many parents to-day?—about to whom, and to what, my first obligations lie!"

As I walk down the Euston Road, I notice with relief that in spite of the crater yawning in the highway, the clean red walls of Friends' House still confront, undamaged, the broad thoroughfare which links so many military objectives. I am glad that Hitler's bombers have so far missed the imperturbable Quaker members of its staff, who stand on the roof at midnight and watch red horror descending on London with a serene courage that few of us can achieve. Perhaps the Lord has gone out of his way to preserve these tranquil doers of his will, whose unshaken philosophy of love and compassion has survived so many wars, and will outlast this.

At Endsleigh Street I join a friend who is driving me to a conference in Cambridge. As we pass the wreck of a large commercial building, and the ruins of small innocent homes in Hampstead and Golder's Green, I meditate upon the change in danger perspectives which the Blitzkrieg has brought even to a generation whose normal lives have been far from secure. Just as age-perspectives alter as one grows older, so the alarm caused by moderate danger decreases when one has experienced its more acute varieties.

Once, I remember, I was alarmed by travelling by aeroplane from Paris to London, and even more by the prospect of flying to the United States in the American Clipper. I was, in fact, greatly relieved when bad winter weather caused Pan-American Airways itself to cancel the flight. My generation is not naturally air-minded; its childhood coincided with the years in which the motor-car seemed, as a method of transport, the most revolutionary invention that man ever made. But to-day, after I have witnessed and all but fallen victim to the devastation caused by military aircraft, the perils of civilian flying seem the creation of a ludicrous timidity, and a Clipper journey to America suggests a measure of security comparable to the progress of a rapid perambulator. The traveller crossing the Atlantic by the Clipper is probably indeed safer now than the average English child being wheeled by its mother to the local park.

When we reach the woods, vivid with orange chestnuts and golden sycamores, which border the roads through the verdant fenlands, I have lived again through the six weeks of bombardment which London's civilians have experienced from Tilbury in the east to Ealing in the west, from Hendon in the north to Wimbledon in the south. Ever since the second week of September, the sirens have wailed all day and the nightly raid has started earlier each evening, until, after five weeks, it now begins

at seven P.M. When the all-clear sounds an hour before
twilight, London's hot-water-loving citizens make a swift
and universal calculation: "Can I get through my bath
before the all-night siren goes?" Usually, in my own experience, one doesn't quite manage it; one is half dry
when the familiar shriek echoes across the city, and
lucky if one has reached the basement with one's cum-
bersome equipment before the bombs begin to fall.

I remember the first fortnight of astonished confusion,
when the relentless rain of high-explosive and delayed-
action bombs caused whole areas to be evacuated and
roped off for days. I recall the letters which took nearly
a week to reach one London district from another, because post offices, like banks, were bombed and removed
to alternative branches—themselves handicapped by ar-
rears of work due to the late arrival and early departure
of clerks who required from three to five hours to travel
between their offices and their homes in the suburbs.
Can I ever make Martin understand that his letters went
astray because, for nearly a fortnight, our correspondence
could neither be received at the customary post office,
nor be delivered to the usual address?

No wonder, I reflect, that in the early period when every
shop and office closed for the entire duration of an alarm,
telegram and trunk calls were refused by post offices, and
toll-calls were obtainable only by booking them two hours
in advance! I recollect my vain attempts to make contact
with friends or business acquaintances whose telephone
exchanges had been bombed or removed; the expenditure,
sometimes, of two or three hours, in which neighbouring
time-bombs went off with alarming explosions, before it
was possible finally to discover that the desired line was
out of action.

In those days—and how often since?—persons and offices within walking distance could be reached most speedily by the use of our feet. On longer journeys, picking up a taxi, we made wearisome detours round barricaded streets; or drove between growing heaps of debris in the endeavour to reach our destination before the siren sounded again, the office closed, and we were swept reluctantly into a public shelter. More than any other experience during the early Blitzkrieg, these hazardous expeditions renewed the sense of playing a diabolical game of musical chairs, in which pure chance determined whether or not we were near our objective when the critical moment came. I hope that future historians will chronicle the part played in the Battle of Britain by London's taxi-drivers, who have constantly braved death by day and by night, and do not even demand an extra tip for the risks that they take.

Throughout these weeks I have noticed, with gathering surprise, the development of a philosophical attitude on the part of a possession-loving people towards the loss of all that they own. To have avoided becoming a casualty seems, to many of my friends whose houses, libraries, or studios have been destroyed, a matter for gratitude undiminished by resentment. Nevertheless, those of us whose houses still stand have made spasmodic attempts to rescue what we can. I look back upon an afternoon spent, when the time-bomb had exploded, in collecting from my desolate house such valuables as I could remember, while gunfire and fighting aeroplanes banged overhead, and the risk of a bomb or a shell bringing the old house down at any moment reduced me to the mental condition of a Red Cross colleague who seized her fountain pen and left ten pounds under her pillow when the hospital ship *Britannic* was torpedoed in 1917. . . .

I recall hastily packing these treasures—pictures, books, manuscripts, jewellery, even Martin's best suit which he forgot to take to the United States—in light inappropriate suitcases which I carry down to friends in the country, dragging them into trains going west from a crowded terminus whence all the porters who might have helped have long disappeared. Most of us have somehow achieved this personal evacuation of treasures, for furniture removers are harassed with demands, and repositories within a hundred miles of London are crammed from cellar to roof.

In one of last month's newspapers, I remember reading that 2,000 tons of bombs had been dropped on London by September 14th . . . How much more has the capital sustained in another four weeks, I wonder. At dawn on October 13th, London recorded its two hundredth raid, yet shops and offices no longer close when the siren sounds, leaving queues to form and business to accumulate. It is less difficult now to get enough exercise and fresh air than it was when everyone was urged to take cover during a raid, and the bright young things of London had not begun their nightly game of "Playing No Man's Land" by dodging home under sheltering walls between the descending bombs.

Recollections come back to me of early morning walks taken after the all-clear had ended one more nightly onslaught; of waking up, fully dressed, from a comfortless doze in the basement to stroll through the chill dawn loveliness of Regent's Park while incendiary bombs still smouldered on adjacent roofs. I walked there in the early morning of Sunday September 15th, when the newspapers reported that the Nazi forces were ready massed for invasion, and in London we welcomed the sudden rising of a strong, fresh wind. Is the rumour true, I wonder, that invasion was actually attempted and withstood on September 16th? How much those of us who survive this war will have to learn about our own lives when the struggle is over! Like the men on the Western Front between 1914 and 1918, we know what is happening only in our own sector of the battle.

Five days afterwards, on the 21st of October, the news-papers are saying that the battle for London has changed. It is being conducted by the Nazis with new tactics and different aims, which will require fresh inventions, new stratagems, and much endurance from the long-suffering British people.

Certainly London life in October, if less surprisedly dis-organised, has been no less perilous than life in Septem-ber. Driving round the town to deliver a series of urgent letters at offices which would not receive them for days if I sent them by post, I remember the cloudy morning of October 4th, when my friend from Francis Square came up from Surrey to find that a second bomb, dropped just behind the Square railings, had transformed into a deso-late ruin the little Queen Anne house which had been her pride and joy. In the grey stone vase outside the porch, her red geraniums lay wilted and black. The door was blown in, the leaded window panes smashed, the delicate carpet and curtains burned, the ceilings fallen; where meticulous order once reigned, chaos had come.

We rescued some of her possessions from the scorched debris of her bedroom; while she packed them, grimly re-signed, I drove to my bank, reached it just after a warning had sounded, and was compelled by falling shrapnel to spend an hour in its underground shelter. Hurrying to Chelsea when the barrage lifted, I seized the miniature paintings of Richard and Hilary inexplicably overlooked on my previous visit, and returned to my flat while the guns of Central London roared loudly above Hyde Park. Writing letters in the basement half through the noisy night, I felt sick and wearied by the constant presence of danger—a feeling re-emphasised four days later, when a squadron of Nazi airmen suddenly appeared from within a green circle of smoke, and dropped bombs on a city area in the morning rush hour. I was then outside Paddington, and not near the city; but it is a common fallacy in London air-raids to imagine that every bomb dropped is aimed direct at oneself. . . .

To-day it is raining, and wounded London looks shabby and sad. Her spirit is unbroken, but her elegance and comfort are gone. Some parts of the city have temporarily lost the ordinary facilities of civilised living; there are rumours of shelter epidemics, and many children not yet evacuated have been inoculated against diphtheria. All over the metropolitan area, doctors are preparing serum injections which will render their patients immune from typhoid and tetanus. Far down the river, a broken sewer pours into the Thames; its putrid odour is blown by the wind as far west as the Strand.

Early in the morning, when I buy a ticket at Regent's Park station, I find mothers and children already queueing up with cushions and mattresses for their nightly occupation of the Tube, and remember seeing, two days ago, a similar queue outside Golder's Green at eleven A.M. Soon, I reflect, London's poorer population, like melancholy troglodytes, will spend its whole life in the Underground, emerging only for half-an-hour after the morning all-clear to purchase its loaves and its fish-and-chips.

My drive to-day shows me brutal changes in London's

familiar face. Many windows have been damaged in Tottenham Court Road, and several buildings are down in Holborn; many of the streets converging on Piccadilly Circus are gashed and gutted; a large bomb has wrecked the south-west corner of Leicester Square. In Chelsea the King's Road has endured an attack by incendiary bombs which have changed a large garage into a blackened skeleton. Opposite a District Railway station, two big houses belonging to doctors who attended Richard and Hilary as babies are doorless and windowless ruins which nothing but complete rebuilding can restore.

These sinister phantoms of a vanished prosperity share no common quality with the planned demolitions of peacetime; they are ghosts raised by the haphazard onslaughts of modern war, which has selected so large a proportion of historic treasures to make up the sum-total of damage. Do we, I wonder, have the same diabolical fortune in Berlin and Hamburg, or are their priceless memorials so few that our progress is necessarily slower? What has happened to the lovely monuments of Germany's past—to Cologne, to Heidelberg, to the smaller Rhineland cities where Martin and I spent such memorable holidays?

When I look at the damaged face of Westminster Abbey or the blackened shell of St. James's Church, Piccadilly, I am left with only the greater desire that our bombs may spare the Cathedral at Cologne and the Duomo in Florence. Beauty and history, whatever their locality, are the jewels of human civilisation. The malevolent cruelty of twentieth century warfare is increased by man's inability to guard them, for the future of his immortal species, from the destructive devices of mortal nations who happen to be seeking each other's extinction at some given moment of time. . . .

The first battle of London, we are told to-day, has been won by the valour of our pilots and the fortitude of our people. Though savage night attacks will certainly continue, the danger of invasion has passed; soon, through the golden prize of air superiority, we shall carry the war into the heart of the enemy . . .

Some day—how long after that?—we may cease to live dangerously. Peace will return, and with it the opportunity, lost in 1918, to build the new world all over again. Shall we, who proved our valour and fortitude in the days of wrath, find a better use for those qualities when that "next time" comes?

28. BERKSHIRE VILLAGE

In the Berkshire village where I am staying for a time to finish some work which has made little progress in London, the fresh wind blowing over the heath pulls the scarlet leaves from cherry trees and ampelopsis, and the sunshine of these last October days crowns the yellowing sycamores with a halo of light. Behind the village, the tall brick-red water tower stands erect against the ashen sky. From the brambles climbing the hedgerows, the last ripe blackberries fall ungathered because no one now has the sugar to preserve them.

Though Italy is invading Greece, and a new "theatre of war" is bringing death and horror to yet more helpless civilians, nothing but the British bombers and fighters circling like huge insects over the Common suggests by day that the village belongs to a country struggling desperately for its existence against a powerful and ruthless opponent. No sirens sound here except when the wind carries their wail far over the hills from Reading or Basingstoke; there are no highly polished fire-fighting lorries, no shelters, no police cars, no helmeted wardens constantly parading outside the gate. Instead the village guardians occasionally blow their whistles; buckets of sand and stirrup-pumps wait on the householders' top-landings, and zealous members of the Home Guards in their new semi-fitting uniforms scan the evening skies with field-glasses on their return from town.

Yet the lovely tranquil days of this Berkshire country are followed by ominous nights. In spite of the square-towered, ivied church with its twirling weather-vane, and the somnolent Horse and Groom Inn carrying the appropriate trade mark of a scarlet hop leaf, peace, as everywhere in the Home Counties, is only a reassuring camouflage over the face of war. On the tangle of tussocky grass at the crossroads stand wood and barbed-wire barricades, and after sunset the German bombers mumble portentously above the clouds with their too-familiar sound of a heavy automobile slowly climbing a steep mountain road. This village lies on the customary route of the Nazi aeroplanes, known to American journalists as "Hell's Corridor," and we wake in the small hours to the sound of distant crashes, the stutter of machine guns and the bumping of anti-aircraft batteries. On still, clear nights, the heavy thunder of London's barrage echoes down the Thames Valley and across the Berkshire hills. From the horizon we watch the searchlights, like Jacob's ladders, climb the menacing vault of sky, illuminating the dark countryside as they strive to catch the invader in the luminous pool where their beams coalesce.

The population, listening to the story of London's Calvary on its wireless sets, nevertheless appreciates its relative security.

"So they dropped them fire-bombs at B. last night," I hear in the village post office.

"Aye! Shook our windows a bit—but we've got nothing to grumble at here. I'm glad I don't live in London."

"Yes. We've got a lot to be thankful for nowadays, haven't we!"

My hostess's red-brick house backs on to a large tangled garden, where apples, pears and little peaches flourish without encouragement in the early autumn. Late roses, nasturtiums, mauve and pink asters bloom with sturdy resolution amongst the fallen leaves which cover the flower beds on the circular lawn. Since a chain of large sunny attics spreads above the living rooms, the household has undertaken to store a number of trunks filled with possessions belonging to friends from more perilous areas. The evacuated treasures which the family is guarding include a large sheep-dog of noble proportions; he belongs to a friend from a much-bombed district in the South-West. To the salvaged collection I have added a few valuables of my own—diaries and documents, the miniatures of the children, Martin's keys, his jewel case, and his new suit rescued from Chelsea.

One of the attics was the playroom of a little boy and girl who have now gone with their mother to Texas. Their diminutive, brightly painted tables and chairs stand among the hundreds of newly picked apples which cover the floor. When I see them I think of my own children's nursery in Chelsea—and decide to frustrate the painful promptings of memory by going for a walk. In a lane, adjoining the common, I meet a small fair-haired girl ten or eleven years old. She reminds me of Hilary; I smile at her, and she smiles shyly back. The windy sky and the tossing trees look suddenly blurred as I hurry on.

When I walk through the woods, the changing colours of the Berkshire leaves smite my perception as emphati-

cally as the colours of an American October—the gold of
the falling chestnuts, the burnt siena and vermilion of oaks
and brambles; the soft sepia and pale smoke-grey of the
fading bracken, the peacock-green of firs and pines. Remembering the happiness of past American autumns, I am
overcome with nostalgia for the Catskill Mountains, the
Mississippi Valley, the wooded Connecticut hills.

But in the morning—though how temporarily in this
sorrowful island!—the yearning nostalgia goes. Instead, I
fall newly in love with the dewdrops sparkling on the
English gorse, the birds twittering in the rhododendrons,
the faint autumn smell of far-off bonfires, the lacy pattern
of ash-leaves across the grass. In the cloudless azure heaven,
a British aeroplane is flying so high that its distant hum
seems a lullaby, not a menace. The chimneys of little red-
roofed houses are smoking in the chill October air; over
the wet stubbly fields, indigo shadows stretch westward
from the roots of apple trees still golden in the orchards.

For me—and I suspect for most of us—it is this that the
word "England" represents. When, as so often, I am abroad,
and especially in the United States where I contemplate,
overwhelmed, the harsh spectacular outline of its Western
lands, England does not mean for me the government at
Westminster, nor even London's historic landmarks—Westminster Abbey, Big Ben, the Houses of Parliament, St.
Paul's Cathedral—now threatened with annihilation by a
foreign power. It certainly does not signify Winston
Churchill, Stanley Baldwin, Ramsay MacDonald, David
Lloyd George, or whoever may be the political Colossus
of the moment; still less does it mean the Royal family,
now so conscientiously doing its best in circumstances always overwhelming for national figureheads who serve the
State by their continuous performance of expected duties.

Least of all does it stand for government officials, those worthy men and women whose nervous fear of outstepping public opinion has so often resulted in bureaucratic cruelty, and is displayed in the self-protective devotion to "red tape," "passing the buck," and every other conceivable form of the procrastination so peculiarly British.

To a limited degree, England does mean for me the process of British justice, which on two occasions—once at a provincial Assize Court, and once in the Police Court of a London magistrate—I have seen function in a fashion as close to the ideal of human decency as the present stage of our spiritual development can be expected to achieve. It means still more the tolerant endurance of British men and women; their patient amusement in Hyde Park or on Tower Hill when open-air orators proclaim opinions to which they are diametrically opposed; their brave, grumbling stoicism in danger and adversity; their staunch refusal even in maximum peril to become panic-stricken refugees.

But more than all, England for me means the fields and lanes of its lovely country; the misty, soft-edged horizon which is the superb gift to the eyes of this fog-laden island; the clear candour of spring flowers; the flame of autumn leaves; the sharp cracking of fallen twigs on frosty paths in winter. These are the things which, no matter where I may travel, I can never forget; this is the England which will dwell with me until my life's end.

And it is an England which neither the pitiful challenging paranoia of Nazidom nor that of any other invader can destroy. Those who call themselves our enemies may obliterate buildings, annihilate monuments, assassinate men and women; they cannot eliminate the flowers, the trees, the grass, the moist sunny air, the quiet inviolate spirit, of a whole countryside. Cities may vanish in a red fury of smoke and flame, but no conqueror by his bombs and aeroplanes can wholly remove the marks which immemorial centuries have laid upon our land. Whatever the future may bring of hope or despair, of sanity or suffering, of peace or war, the villages of this country will be England for ever.

29. THE RUINS OF TROY

ON A MILD MISTY November morning, my friend from
Berkshire and I stand on Cherry Tree Pier, high above the
Thames in Bermondsey's dockland, and look apprehen-
sively towards the east and the west.

Once this pier must have lain in the depths of wooded
riverside country; perhaps there was a tavern beside it,
and girls dancing under the cherry trees. Now there is
nothing to distinguish it from the piers, wharves, cranes,
and warehouses that lie between the river bank and Jamaica
Road; nothing but the sense, which still persists, of standing far out in mid-stream as though on the top deck of a
ship. Westwards we look across the Pool of London towards the beautiful arch of Tower Bridge, still proudly
intact; eastwards the river curves broadly past Rother-
hithe towards Greenwich and the distant sea. Amongst
the cranes and wharves which stretch along both banks as
far as our eyes can reach, we find, as we grimly expected,
the burnt-out skeletons of warehouses which on many past
nights have lighted the East End sky with their fires, and
guided the raiders in their efforts to destroy the docks.

In the early weeks of the Blitzkrieg, such extensive
parts of these dockland areas were wrecked that the inhabitants who worked in the City or the West End gave

up the fruitless attempt to reach Central London by train or tram, and travelled to their work by water bus. Now the main roads have been cleared, and London Transport has put on an express service of motor buses which replace the slower river steamers. To-day the Thames, deceptively quiet and dimly blue, is empty even of tugs and barges; only the little motor launches of the river police run up and down awaiting the trouble that will certainly make its way along London's chief landmark before the sunny day is out.

A hundred yards eastwards from Cherry Tree Pier stood an old riverside inn, with a wooden balcony extending above the water. Here, a few evenings before he sailed for America, Martin and I drank tankards of ale at sunset, watched twilight eclipse the grey curve of Tower Bridge, and walked back through the darkening narrow streets to his room at the Bermondsey Settlement. To-day the little inn is a heap of wreckage; its bar and its balcony alike have gone, and the flour mill next door has burned to a cinder. Many of the winding passages where we walked are blocked with rubble or barricaded for craters, but behind the smashed fringes of the river London's dockers still whistle as they unload bags of flour from the huge lifting cranes.

Now that the dark foggy nights have come and November gales scream through the Straits of Dover, the autumn bombardment seems to have passed its peak of frightfulness of the capital. So Margaret and I, hiring a little car from a Cockney tobacconist, have decided to see what more we can of the consequences of this Battle of London which already seems to have lasted for so large a part of our lives. Like the men on the Western Front in the First World War, we find it all too easy to follow only what is happening in our own sector of the line. Already, from the damage to the County Hall, the crashed northern wing of St. Thomas's Hospital where young Peter Spilsbury died, the complete demolition of a well-known college, and the gutted black lead factory near the Elephant and Castle, we realise that in the West End we had not seen the half of the battlefield.

As we drive north over Tower Bridge towards Whitechapel and Shoreditch, the familiar banshee note of the siren reverberates loudly from the river. We are looking with interest at the scattering of small debris round the Tower and the marks of attack on the walls of the Royal Mint, when a steel-helmeted policeman stops our car.

"It is my duty," he announces solemnly, "to warn you that an air-raid alarm has sounded."

Our Cockney owner-driver throws him a glance of unutterable contempt.

"Which way's Bethnal Green?" he inquires laconically.

"Two and a half miles to the left," responds the policeman, his obligation as guardian of the reckless public which persists in driving through air-raids now punctually fulfilled. Our chauffeur, we learn later, sleeps imperturbably on the top floor of a small block of Kensington flats which owns no shelter. Aerial torpedoes, and high explosive bombs go off nightly around him without disturbing his poise. Towards the end of the day, showing us the gruesome remains of an entire street wiped out by a huge bomb which fell in the grounds of the Imperial War Museum a few hundred yards from his flat, his voice rings with the satisfaction of an Ancient Mariner describing his particular Battle of Trafalgar.

"Got on me toes when I heard that one, I did!" he tells

us. "Went out to find it, and was there before the A.R.P.
crowd themselves!"

He goes on to give us grisly details of casualties dug
out by a detachment of troops from the wreckage of surface shelters destroyed by a direct hit in his neighbourhood. The possibility of becoming, in some future raid,
another such casualty appears to disturb him not at all.

"Unless it has me name on it, it won't git me," he affirms, typical of the fatalistic Londoner in his belief that
destiny remains unaffected by caution. The numerous
"crumps" which have occurred in his district inspire him
with pride rather than apprehension, and he repudiates
firmly the suggestion that any other London borough
might have produced a longer roll of casualties than his.

We drive on through the air-raid down Whitechapel
Road. The appearance of the Mile End Road, into which
we run after negotiating a huge smash where the two
thoroughfares join, suggests that not one London raid
could have occurred without a bomb or two dropping directly upon it; but this morning the wrecked street remains
quiet, and we hear no warning explosive sounds. As we
reach Bow from Stepney and Whitechapel, I reflect lugubriously on the similarity of debris wherever it is found.
Whether the crashed building stood in Bow Road or in
Berkeley Square, its damp, blackened ruins equally suggest that nothing worth saving was kept in the house.

At a corner close to Bow Road Station, the wreckage of
a mission hall wears a conspicuous placard:

BOMBED BUT STILL CARRYING ON.

We notice with relief that, though the famous bells are
silenced, the small architectural jewel which is Bow Church

still faces undamaged the wide tragic street with the gentle innocence of a nursery rhyme invented in a kinder and simpler age. A hundred yards or so further on, a wide area of industrial ruin barely concealed by hurriedly erected hoardings is marked—with intentional humour? we wonder—by a large rough notice-board:

THIS FREEHOLD SITE FOR DISPOSAL.

On the other side of Bow Bridge over the River Lee, the car suddenly reaches a square half-mile of devastation so complete that even our damage-accustomed eyes examine it with a fixed stare of incredulity. All life, all semblance of human habitation, has disappeared from these crushed and flattened acres; the place is a No Man's Land, a Naboth's Vineyard, a burnt and blackened Limbo containing the foul rubbish of an exploded civilisation.

The driver, his comprehensive knowledge of London defeated by the sinister metamorphosis, beckons one of the khaki-uniformed members of the Auxiliary Military Pioneers who are digging among the ruins.

"Where's this?" he inquires peremptorily.

"Old Ford Road," briefly replies the conscripted student of East End archaeology. A moment later, we pass a railway station, still hopefully announcing "Trains to All Parts." Beyond the station, the surviving skeleton of a former wall is labelled with equal optimism: "Factory Premises to Let." As we run into Bethnal Green, the pile of debris that confronts us provokes even our imperturbable driver to comment.

"That was a naughty one!" he murmurs, a suspicion of wry amusement mingled even with his evident sympathy for those fellow-Cockneys who have suffered such severe devastation. Instinctively I look into the sky to see whether any more "naughty ones" are preparing to demolish the car, but I perceive only the barrage balloons, swinging like white iridescent pearls against the pale cobalt-blue sky. I am still tentatively regarding them, when the steady booming note of the all-clear assures me that someone else's air-raid is over.

In Stepney we drive past the defaced church of St. Benet's into Globe Road—another wrecked area comparable to the Western Front in 1918. Outside the gutted remnants of a boys' school, the few remaining surface shelters carry posters issued by the Ministry of Health, urging the mothers of the borough to evacuate their children to the country without delay. No one can now allege that the Ministry has not done its best to battle with the peculiar ignorant obstinacy of a surviving type of London parent which still persists in taking its young children each night into the germ-infested atmosphere of the Underground and allowing them to play amongst the ruins by day. The only remaining measure is compulsory evacuation—and Malcolm MacDonald, the much-tried son of Ramsay, has already wearily explained over the radio that if this expedient were attempted the London police would not be sufficient to deal with the offenders, nor the London prisons large enough to hold them.

We are running now from the East End towards the City, through the Hackney Road and Bethnal Green. I am glad to see the great church of St. John-on-Bethnal-Green still standing intact at the crossroads, though there is a huge chip on the face of the clock. Nearly all London's larger clocks have suffered from shock or from splinters; they were not erected to withstand the onslaught of barrage and bombs. As we pass them we find undamaged the Queen's Hospital for Children and St. Botolph's Church in Bishopsgate, though Cornhill is marked "No Entry," and many windows in St. Peter-on-Cornhill are shattered. A wrecked acre surrounds the Monument, but the white pointer of the tall column itself still stands unspoiled.

As we reach Ludgate Hill, the usual grey pigeons with green necks and pink feet are walking placidly round the rescued Colossus of St. Paul's Cathedral. There is, I believe, no Londoner to-day who could look on the surviving black and grey dome and share the emotional detachment of the pigeons. We stare incredulously at the still barricaded crater where the one-ton time-bomb fell, just missing the structure itself. Leaving the car, we are driven by an irresistible impulse of gratitude towards Providence and Lieutenant Davies' bomb-removing squadron up the wide stone steps and through the one door still open to the public.

We move slowly along the black and white floor, like a gigantic draughts-board in intermittent sunshine. Iron scaffolding has been erected round the Duke of Wellington's tomb, but the black marble sarcophagus of Lord Melbourne and his family is still protected only by its confident inscription: "Through the Gate of Death we pass to our Joyful Resurrection." Close by, the gentle features of Sir Joshua Reynolds' statue look with troubled compassion towards the wrecked High Altar, as though oppressed by the passionate human stupidity which, with the ruthlessness of an angry child, smashes the very treasures that in rational moods it values the most.

The shattered fragments of the High Altar still lie where they fell, strangely lit up by the sunlight which streams through the surrounding gloom straight on to the white remnants of stone. There are jagged holes in the stained-glass windows above the Altar and a gap shows in the roof torn by the bomb, but the crucified Christ, with arms outstretched, looks down undamaged upon the debris in sorrowful pity for the sins of the world. Standing face to face with the carven steadfastness of the merciful Son of Man, I read a square white card on which is printed a Prayer for Protection Against Air-Raids:

"Almighty and most merciful God, Who dwellest not in temples made with hands: Be Thou the guardian, we beseech Thee, of our churches and our homes; Keep this Thy House in peace and safety; and grant that all who worship here may find their refuge under the shadow of Thy wings, and serve Thee with a quiet mind; through Jesus Christ our Lord. Amen."

Silently we leave St. Paul's and drive towards Fleet Street through familiar corners of the City. In St. Martin-le-Grand, a large business office has been demolished; Smithfield Market is carrying on its work amid damage from bombs; the exquisite grace of Charterhouse Square, where leaves are falling upon the surface shelters which cover the garden, ignores the gaping ugly wound left by the collapse of a corner building. As we drive through Farringdon Street, our driver tells us that the *Evening Standard* had a bomb through its lift-shaft which damaged several offices, but in Fleet Street, though Anderton's Hotel has vanished, the buildings belonging to the *Daily Telegraph*, the *Daily Express*, and the *News of the World* stand still unbombed. Driving slowly towards the Strand, we stop with suddenly laboured breath before the blackened shell beneath the surviving white guardian tower which was once the loveliest of London's City churches, St. Clement Danes.

There is no end, here, to the grim tale of ruin. The inside of the church has been gutted by fire, the stone fabric defaced by splinters, the windows broken and their beautiful frames twisted into a grotesque travesty of the carver's skill. The church clock, which has stopped at ten minutes to seven, indicates the early evening hour of the raid. With its back to the eastern wing, the statue of Samuel Johnson, facing Fleet Street, still stands unharmed among the charred leaves and branches of a demolished tree, the sardonic eyes fixed on a book, the right hand raised in portentous exhortation. On the blackened wall of the church a large poster has been pasted:

HIT BACK
with
WAR SAVINGS
and
STOP THIS

It seems, perhaps, more appropriate to the damaged corner of the Law Courts and the shattered windows of Clement's Inn across the street, than to a house, however cruelly damaged, which was once dedicated to the service of a Master who left for all time the response of love to its would-be destroyers: "Father, forgive them, for they know not what they do."

In Trafalgar Square we observe with thankfulness that St. Martin-in-the-Fields is still intact, though a huge crater shows where a recent bomb damaged the Underground. We drive past Wyndham's Theatre, which is running a show appropriately named "Diversion." The Soho Hospital for Women still stands, but the wreckage of the Saville Theatre and its adjacent street resembles the Western Front as closely as the Old Ford Road. In one thoroughfare a pile of debris still covers the spot where many brave men lost their lives, and only the ribs of the roof and the small turretlike tower remain to remind Londoners of the beauty which was once St. Anne's Church, Soho.

Through ruined areas in Gower Street and Tottenham Court Road, we return for lunch to my flat, sad and disheartened by the loss of the past which had been, from childhood, an integral part of our lives. It is not a peaceful luncheon; another air-raid starts as we reach the doorway, and even before we go down to the restaurant, we see the formation of enemy planes flash silver in the sun. Again, as so often, they fight noisily above our heads as we sit at our meal, and when we return upstairs the pale afternoon sky is streaked with the white filmy lines which mark the field of aerial battle.

A new journey takes us out to the Western areas of London, already more familiar than the East. The house in Piccadilly where the King lived as Duke of York has been deprived of its back rooms and the nurseries where the young princesses played, but Hyde Park Corner and Knightsbridge have lost no landmarks.

"The Oratory's all right!" I exclaim with relief as we run up the Brompton Road, for after the fate of the City churches the intact appearance of any large church seems a matter for surprise. Kensington, I find, has suffered severely since my last visit to Francis Square; the circular walls of the Albert Hall are blackened and its windows have gone, and boarding replaces most of the glass in the front of John Barker's store. Beside the familiar corner of Kensington High Street and the Earl's Court Road, we stop to look sadly at the skeleton of Our Lady of Victories —a loss to the Catholics as grievous as St. Clement Danes and St. Anne's, Soho, to the Protestants. Beyond the graceful front arch which still stands erect, the demolished roof is open to the sky, the floor covered with burned and blackened rafters. Inside the shattered porch, a small blue-robed statuette of Our Lady holds the Child in her arms. The inscribed card beside her does not echo the angry defiance of St. Clement Danes:

> Blessed Virgin
> Mary
> This is my Church.
> Have Pity

We wander silently up the leaf-covered footpath of Holland Walk to see ruined Holland House, of which the newspapers have written so much, but from a distance the big mansion shows little conspicuous trace of damage. The work of the raiders seems more apparent in the shattered trees of the Park, the smashed back windows of large adjacent houses, the demolished front gate where huge lumps of red brick and fragments of the wrought-iron gateway have been flung as though by a giant earthquake across the garden.

Francis Square, I find, has been bombed yet again; in my friend's house are cheerful young workmen, singing in the midst of desolation as they replace the boards blown away from the gaps where doors and windows have been. Not only the geraniums but the stone vase which held them has now been hit; its fragments lie scattered over the small front garden. The room where I slept, again swept by fire, is blacker than before. From its windows I look down upon the once exquisite paved flower garden at the back of the house; the creeper carefully trained to grow up the stone stairway leading from the garden to the sunny balcony where I used to write has fallen away, scorched and dry, like an old torn veil. Already coarse weeds choke the crevices between the flagstones, and have stolen the flower-beds from the dying asters and gladioli.

We drive on to Chelsea past demolished studios and burnt-out garages. My sad empty house, at the eastern end of our terrace, still stands erect, but the dust inside lies thicker than ever, and an incendiary bomb has burned a hole through the stone floor of an upstairs balcony. The western section of the terrace, which lies close to an industrial area, has tumbled into dust as completely as though no half-dozen old houses had ever stood there. Before the wide bay made here by the river, Turner's House—one of Chelsea's most cherished possessions, where the artist painted his London sunsets—has been transformed by fire and steel into a squalor of desolation never imagined by his prosperous, complacent era which was preparing, even then, the road to our Calvary.

It is time now to drive homewards along the Embankment, where the bridges still span the river but many houses near them are shattered. As we return to the famous streets in which twilight is already lurking, we realise that we have been looking at the ruins of London for more than five hours. We both confess to feeling tired and stiff, and a little dazed by the visible story of havoc that we have seen.

In Westminster, we knew that we should find parts of the Abbey defaced, the windows smashed in St. Margaret's Church, the ancient stone fabric of Westminster Hall scarred by bombs which have ravaged the base of Cœur de Lion's statue, and bent the upright defiance of his lifted sword. Whitehall, too, has endured the fury of the bombers; in many Ministries windows are broken, and debris lies at the entrance to Downing Street. Still untouched amid so much damage, the Cenotaph to "The Glorious Dead" of the last World War mocks their confident faith that they were preventing the next. For the hundredth time during this strange melancholy day, I wonder whether mankind will learn, even from a war which has wrecked its homes and destroyed its children, the lessons that loom like reproachful ghosts from the record of its past.

What is it, I ask myself, of which this long journey through the devastated areas of my own city has reminded me? Suddenly my memory leaps back over nineteen years, and I recollect driving, for many hours of an autumn day, round the ruined villages of the Somme in 1921.

Winifred was with me then, Margaret is with me now; and at first sight, perhaps, there is little in common between the shattered streets of the world's greatest capital and those ruined agricultural townlets. Yet the impression left upon me by both journeys through the wreckage of a civilisation is much the same, though the strange sense of repeated experience is not explained by the peculiar resemblance between damaged houses robbed of their roofs and ravaged trees deprived of their branches. Nor is it due to the fact that the Old Ford Road, like the demolished villages of Hébuterne and Villers-Bretonneux, had to be labelled before I or anyone who knew it better, could have recognised the district as its former self.

The linked memories are rather those of Amiens Cathedral, where in 1921 we started our journey by looking at the still boarded windows smashed by German shells, and the crucified Christ gazing down in compassionate grief upon the sunlit ruins of St. Paul's High Altar. Though nineteen years have intervened between the two tragic pilgrimages, the emotion that remains is again neither anger nor resentment, but only an everlasting sorrow, and a passionate pity which I still have not learned how best to use or express.

30. FOR EVER LONDON

IN THE NINE CENTURIES which have passed since the Norman Conquest, London has known four major catastrophes.

The first—a fire in the year of William Rufus's accession to the throne—destroyed St. Paul's Cathedral and gutted the primitive city around it. The second and third came in two successive years six centuries later. The second—the Great Plague of 1665—left seventy thousand dead to be buried in pits and covered with quicklime; the third—the Great Fire of 1666—took all but one-fifth of the walled medieval city. London, rebuilt, with many of her beautiful churches designed by Christopher Wren, believed that she had outlived the age in which man remained at the mercy of pestilence and fire.

But her fourth calamity began, after four more centuries, on September 7, 1940. That night, from different angles, at different heights and with different speeds, came fifteen hundred aeroplanes of all types and sizes, dropping bombs by the ton in eight hours of terror, making nonsense of optimistic newspaper assertions that the former reconnaissance fliers were mere "nuisance raiders" designed to give London's citizens insomnia. Furious fires, climbing the midnight sky from slums and docks, destroyed in a moment the simple precaution of the black-

213

out; refugees from the bombed areas took shelter in the sophisticated hotels of Central London; civilians listening in shelters and basements to the ceaseless roar of the planes and the intermittent thud of the bombs, lost all sense of time, of order, even of consciousness. That night, at least four hundred people perished; on the next, two hundred died and eight hundred were injured. No one then knew whether, in loss of life or material damage, the Blitzkrieg would equal the Great Plague and the Great Fire. But everyone realised that, in the impression made upon the consciousness of the waiting, watching, listening world, this fourth disaster—no "act of God," but the deliberate work of mankind which had not achieved the moral power to control the instruments of its own invention—was greater than the former three combined. London, bombed, burned, and battered, became for two months the suffering symbol of England's anguish, and a living sacrifice to the spiritual failure of the race of men.

On a week-end in November, the newspapers which for eight weeks have alternately warned Londoners against disaster, pleaded with them for patience and urged them to endurance, suddenly begin to strike a different note. A London evening paper publishes a leading article entitled "The Nameless Victory." It speaks of the three clear days for which, in the autumn of 1805, Napoleon prayed in order that he might accomplish the invasion of England; it records the sudden energy and decision with which he turned his back on the English Channel and marched eastwards to his victories at Austerlitz and Jena; it asserts that, despite these conquests, Napoleon lost his chance of world domination when he left his camp at Boulogne and abandoned to Britain the opportunity to repair her strength.

Then, with quiet dignity, it produces the comparison for which this introduction has prepared the reader.

"Another nameless victory has been scored in this war, and we have the power, if we choose, to turn it to decisive advantage. The triumph of our airmen has thrown Hitler back from these coasts. He may still contemplate invasion, but he knows now that he can never make it in the circumstances of his choice, with our air force beaten from the skies. Like Napoleon he has been forced to look eastward for his compensation. . . . Let us bear ourselves as a nation which has won a great victory."

The next day, a Sunday newspaper publishes figures which show us that, in terms of aeroplane losses alone, the Blitzkrieg has been checked. The German Air Force, we learn—and even the most sceptical reader knows the care with which the British Fighter Command checks its figures—has lost 3 aircraft and 14 airmen for every one of ours. Since August 8th, when massed attacks began upon our coasts, the Nazis have lost 2,433 bombers and fighters in almost equal numbers, and over 6,000 airmen killed or taken prisoner. The cold figures exonerate the imagination of all but a few from picturing that weight of crashed and blackened metal, and from contemplating the agonies of those burned and shattered men. In the same period, we read, the British Fighter Command has lost only 353 pilots. To the wives and mothers of those young fliers, the word "only" will bring no comfort; but the rest of us can justly compare them, not merely with the Nazi losses, but with the 70,000 "Missing of the Somme" commemorated at Thiepval—the men never found or never identified, whose numbers were added to the longer list of known casualties in one great battle of infantry warfare.

The weekly figures, we are told, show a gradual weakening of the German effort in spite of constant changes in tactics. Mentally recapitulating our own activities on each of the historic days recorded, we follow the details of the leading battles. On August 8th, when London was still pitying the South Coast and thinking itself the safest place in the country, the Nazi losses in three mass dive-bombing attacks made on convoys and harbours were 24 Junkers, 87 dive-bombers, 36 Messerschmitt 110's, and 109 fighters. A week later, on August 15th, when I stood in the main-line terminus and watched the trains running placidly southward in spite of "mishaps," 1,000 German bombers and fighters launched upon England the biggest attack in the history of air fighting. Instead of enabling Hitler to celebrate the conquest of London, they lost 180 aircraft that day, and 472 bombers and fighters during the next seven days—a record number of losses for one week. It was then that Germany gave up the use of the Junker dive-bomber which she had hitherto regarded as her deadliest weapon.

The opening night of London's Blitzkrieg, September 7th, is a date that for personal as well as national reasons I can never forget. Had I been numbered with the six thousand casualties of that week of terror, it would not now matter to me that the mass visitation of fifteen hundred raiders in eight hours cost the Nazis 103 crashed aeroplanes. The second major attempt by the Luftwaffe to crush the Fighter Command defences occurred, I learn, on September 15th—the sunny London Sunday on which I walked in Regent's Park soon after dawn, and at night slept with the soundness of deep fatigue through several hours of heavy gunfire. That day the Germans lost the record number of 185 aircraft—a figure reduced only to 133 in the last great battle of September 27th, when the proportion of fighter escorts to bombers was four to one. Now, it seems, bombers have almost been abandoned, for the present, and the Nazis are sending over high-flying Messerschmitts which can carry only small loads of bombs.

At the end of October, a new phase of the war began in the Mediterranean. Now, in November, we realise that another main theatre of conflict has opened, and that England's hour, though far from over, has witnessed the determined survival of this island. We shall still be attacked; more precious buildings will be destroyed, more lives of unoffending citizens ended; but, judged by military facts alone, the Battle for Britain has been won by the British, and the Battle for London through the refusal of Londoners to descend to panic. By aerial valour, by military fortitude, by unremitting civilian endurance, the people of England have kept the use of their country for themselves.

Never again—provided only that we have the wisdom to play a nobler part than that of 1919 in making the peace which must one day come—need Britain pass through a crisis equal to the months of September and October, 1940. If half the courage and ingenuity displayed in winning the Battle for London had been used in a decade-long effort to eliminate the most barbarous weapons of war, those weeks of hell, with all that they have cost us, need never have occurred. Cannot besotted humanity at last apply the moral to its future?

There are some, it seems, who neither will nor can. In the same Sunday newspaper which claims, by a sober publication of figures, that Britain has already won her defensive victory, a signed leading article inquires: "Can We Forgive?" The writer speaks of the ruin to priceless

London buildings whose worth cannot be measured by economic values, but in terms of their significance to the national spirit; of the ruthless blows dealt by Nazidom to the treasure-house of the Empire's love and faith. Human beings, he explains, can be given protection or moved to safer areas, but neither expedient is possible for churches, halls, and museums whose life is enshrined in the glory of glass and stone. In consequence thirty-two London churches—amongst them a number of Wren's masterpieces—have been wholly or partially destroyed; forty-seven seriously damaged; many more injured and defaced. With them we have lost, not dead monuments, but a part of the centuries which have gone to make England herself. It is this ruthless destruction of our history, concludes the writer, that we cannot forgive.

And I sympathise. Tears come into my eyes when I recall the grotesque transformation of lovely St. Clement Danes, the windowless arches of Westminster Hall, the roofless shell of Our Lady of Victories, the ugly fire-scarred ruin that was Turner's House in Cheyne Walk. We cannot compensate ourselves by dreaming—as scientific contributors to the daily newspapers have already begun to dream—of the fine modern city that we shall one day build on the ruins of the old. Fine modern cities which we are not likely to rival have been built elsewhere; they have arisen superlatively in New York, in Chicago, in San Francisco after the earthquake. Nothing can cure the heartbreak which we suffer from having—in the vivid words of the American news-magazine *Time* —"the past bombed out of our lives."

It is relevant here, perhaps, to inquire what we ourselves have destroyed in Cologne, in Hamburg, in Frankfort and Munich; what Germany has to forgive us who centuries ago, by our Balance of Power policy, committed Europe to ceaseless national conflict. Policies as well as buildings are historic; we must not forget that. But in London there are more records of the past to annihilate than in any German city except, perhaps, Vienna; and the hours available for raids to our opponents, owing to their two thousand miles of coast so close to our shores, have been at least three times longer than our own hours of attack. If ever we Londoners were entitled to bitterness, it is for the loss of the history which was ours centuries before William I of Germany created modern Berlin with its gilded Reichstag and is boastful mile of Sieges-Allee.

It is none the less true that London could not be destroyed even if the damage done were far greater than that of the present. Nor is she indestructible only because so much more of her is left than we ever dreamed we could save when the Blitzkrieg started; because, though streets have collapsed into rubble and famous buildings are gone, her familiar silhouette remains unaltered. Leaning at sunset over the wide arches of Westminster Bridge, we can still look lovingly upon the city that appears as an old engraving delicately etched against a tranquil sky. The cranes, though some are now charred ghosts, still lift their pinnacles above the Pool of London; the pigeons walk serenely around St. Paul's, and the seabirds flap their wide grey wings over the ancient barges in the Bay at Chelsea. But London's immortality lies not only in these eternal things; the spirit of men and women from generation to generation matters even more than they. It is my faith in my countrymen which makes me repeat the question, "Can we forgive?" and try to supply a different answer.

I believe that we must indeed forgive; that if we do not, we shall sacrifice an essential part of our national quality. "A nation," affirms our leader-writer, "cannot watch its holiest monuments being battered, with system and premeditation, and then meet the enemy afterwards in a forgiving, tolerant spirit." Can it not? If not, then it has already lost the peace; and if it loses yet another peace, the war of 1965 will annihilate our children and our London too.

It is true that our churches stand, or should stand, "for the belief of men in themselves and each other and in the God of their worship"; but that God himself made forgiveness the keystone of the faith which he founded. If Nazidom indeed strikes deliberately, as a dangerous lunatic might strike, at this conception of religion and the treasure-houses which enshrine it, our opponents merit more compassion for their false and cruel values than for the political wrongs which they have transformed into a perverted crusade. This peculiar manifestation of evil will neither be cured nor be driven from the world by our imitative adoption of its standards.

Since the founder of our faith could forgive his destroyers for the loss of his life, shall we not seek to forgive our destroyers for the ruin of our past? If we fail in forgiveness, something that is for ever England, and for ever London, will have departed from our land. It is the spirit of the British Tommy who gave his cigarettes to his wounded opponent in the German prisoners' ward of a British Army hospital at Étaples in 1917, with the half-apologetic explanation: "Poor Jerry, he can't help it!"

The majority of my countrymen, like all people who are guileless and semi-informed, can be roused by propaganda to vindictiveness and hatred. They were so roused at the end of 1918; they could be roused again to-day, though the half defiant, half amused attitude of Cockney Londoners towards the raiders who rob them of sleep and bomb them out of their homes does not yet suggest any passionate thirst for vengeance. But the essence of the British character is a desire to live and let live; to judge not, that it be not judged; to pity its enemies rather than to condemn.

This spirit, though it explains so much of our inertia, is also our greatest historic treasure; a treasure which matters more to humanity's future than even St. Paul's Cathedral or Westminster Abbey. On a Friday morning in November, 1940, I found in St. Paul's itself a noble recognition of the fact that in the growth of compassion, of love, and of forgiveness, lies London's best hope of immortality.

EPILOGUE

As I STOOD in St. Paul's Cathedral and saw how the image of the crucified Christ looked down in pity upon the shattered remnants of his Altar, the friend who had come with me put into my hand a little booklet which she had taken from a table beside the aisle. Glancing at it as we left the Cathedral, I saw that it was entitled: "The First Year of War. A Review and a Rededication."

I did not look at the booklet again until late that evening. I expected, I humbly confess, to find the customary ecclesiastical propaganda about the holiness of this war, the righteousness of our cause, and the necessity of our victory if the impeccable standards of the British Empire were to prevail throughout the world. It was, therefore, with the more astonishment that I turned from the first section called "Thanksgiving" to a second entitled "Penitence."

"Some people," I read with the eagerness of rising hope, "are inclined to deprecate penitence as tending to weaken our conviction of the justice of our cause and our resolve to achieve victory. The answer to that is clear. Only cowardice, hypocrisy or a bad conscience makes men afraid to know the truth about themselves. If we are to ask for God's help we must do so on his terms; his terms are: 'Ye shall know the truth, and the truth shall make you free.' Let us therefore acknowledge with sincerity and humility the truths about our national sins and weaknesses which war has laid bare.

"We had sought for peace, but did not know or would not face the price which must be paid for having it. We tried to *keep* peace rather than to *make* it.

"We had prided ourselves on our empire, but had begun to lose our strength and honour because we had put power and wealth before responsibility and duty.

"We had set ourselves to achieve recovery, prosperity and security, but they were to be for ourselves, our nation, or even for some classes and sections within our nation, rather than for mankind.

"We had perverted the true order of human life, by making wealth and profit, rather than the satisfaction of human need, the aim of our industry and commerce.

"We had been blind to the continuance of needless suffering and waste in human life.

"We had forgotten God, and believed that we could build a better world by our own skill and effort."

I read on. I was less surprised now to find, under "Intercession," a series of prayers for the peoples of Europe and her refugees which did not exclude their oppressors from "the common need of mankind, bewildered, frightened, embittered, led astray by delusions which end in despair." Finally I turned, in the last section called "Dedication," to a series of prayers which left me penitently grateful for the renewed power of the Church to point to the way of life which its Master laid down:

"We have seen something of what God is doing for us and asking of us. We have seen the exposure of our past failures: we have seen the distress and confusion to which

our common sin has brought us all. In the light of these
things let us turn again to God, and offer to him the life
of this nation asking him to make it such that it can be
the instrument of his purpose.

"Let us pray that he will use us, if it be his will, as the
means through which the domination of force and false-
hood is broken, and mankind set free to build a new
way of life.

"That he will teach us what it costs to be so used, and
make us willing to pay that cost . . .

"From boastfulness and pride: from the refusal to
acknowledge our need of God.

"From bitterness and vindictiveness against our enemies, from persecution or suspicion of refugees and aliens.

"From surrender of freedom in speech and thought:
from making expediency the test of truth and right.

"From cowardice and selfishness: from seeking to escape our share of hardship, or making profit out of the
need of others.

"Good Lord deliver us. . . .

"Let us dedicate the life of this nation and our own
lives, in suffering or in security, in success or in reverses,
to the doing of God's will and the service of mankind.

"Here, O Lord, we offer and present unto thee ourselves, our souls and bodies, to be a continual sacrifice
unto thee. We beseech thee to take us as we are, and of
thy mercy make us what thou wouldst have us be: through
Jesus Christ our Lord."

As a nation we can, I believe, best help the fulfilment
of this prayer by studying humbly and honestly—not
when peace is made, or in the following decades, but *now*
—the causes of the present conflict. By this I do not mean

the process of mutual destruction which we hear described *ad nauseam* over the radio, nor the political events of the past eight years. War is no longer a concentrated manoeuvre carried out by opposing armies in a limited area. It is not even a process of mutual bombing, but an enormous illimitable struggle, fought with economic and political weapons reinforced by the perverted ingenuity of countless human minds. Its causes lie deep, not only in history, but in the conflict of traditions, assumptions, beliefs, and values which compose the complex creatures whom we recognise as ourselves.

There are few, I imagine, possessed of any capacity for thought who do not repudiate the pathetic popular simplification of this war as "all due to one man"—though that man is responsible for certain of its features. No catastrophe of such a size could be due to one man, one nation, or even one epoch; its origins must be sought in convulsive historic forces which are themselves the products of spiritual maladjustment. Every attempt to find a starting point must result in the arbitrary selection of a date.

Many of us are sadly aware that the fiercest problems of the present age, whether international, national, or merely personal, have been caused by the degree to which material development and scientific invention have outstripped man's knowledge of his own nature and his power to control it. This outpacing of moral by intellectual capacity is a phenomenon of the past two centuries and especially of the last fifty years.

We ourselves invented the instruments which make modern warfare so diabolical—the chemical industry begun in the Victorian age; the aeroplane which could have been used for the unification of the world and the saving of life, but instead has been converted into the

cruelest vehicle of destruction ever conceived by perverted genius; the tank which has turned the roads of
Europe into pathways of blood. We did not invent but
have done much to further the development of broadcasting, which might have increased knowledge and
brought distant peoples into friendly contact, but instead
has become the insidious servant of competitive propaganda, warping human integrity by the falsification or
suppression of the truth. Three out of these four inventions could already have united mankind and enlarged
human life. Instead, through lack of moral power and the
bankruptcy of statesmanship, they have been turned to
the erasing of a civilisation.

Since war begins, in the first instance, within the individual soul, the widespread exploration of the human
mind and a deeper examination of the sources of human
conduct—tasks now undertaken only by a handful of
specialists—may ultimately lead to a way of escape from
our present dilemma. The scientific development of those
moral values which have now fallen so far behind mechani-
cal progress would have its repercussions on every kind
of social phenomenon. It would affect legal practice, penal
administration and medical treatment. Many afflictions
hitherto regarded as purely physical would be traced to
mental disease or nervous obsession, and the patient
would be sent to the psychoanalyst instead of to the
surgeon.

This extended field of knowledge would cut at the roots
of war by throwing light on the motives which make
nations turn to physical conflict though alternative solu-
tions exist, and cause individual citizens to accept it even
though it destroys or impairs all that they value most
dearly in life. We should perceive more clearly the devastating effect of crude military operations upon the more

civilised and constructive sections of the community. Finally we should realise that nations, which are only collections of personalities, respond in precisely the same fashion as individuals to challenge and provocation; and like individuals can be healed by patience, pity and understanding.

But if we go back beyond our two centuries of scientific and industrial development, we shall perceive that the outpacing of man's benevolent moral power by his malevolent intellect is itself not a cause but a symptom of his failure. We may say with partial truth that this war, like the last, began at some period between the Renaissance and the nineteenth century, when the idea of imperialism, born from the voyages of the Great Discoverers, brought some nations earlier than others into the race for empire. We can go yet further back, and find its explanation in the European national struggles of the fourteenth and fifteenth centuries. More correctly still, we can say that it started when Christianity was adopted as the official religion of the Roman Empire, and the Christian Church lost its spiritual force by compromise with the State.

For this war, like all wars, can only be truthfully explained in terms of the age-old struggle between the ideal of power, which is essentially political, and the ideal of love, which inspired many oriental religions but found its most vital expression in the teaching of Christ. Until we recognise the length and magnitude of that struggle, the perpetual war of individual liberty against state totalitarianism will never be won nor even effectively waged, since its weapons are not bombs and machine guns, but the spear of the mind and the sword of the spirit.

The adoption of Christianity by the Roman Empire was an attempt to compromise between the two ideals. But as love and power are wholly incompatible sources of inspiration, and obedience to the latter is far easier and more materially profitable, that compromise represented a victory for the ideal of power which has dominated world history ever since, and is finding its logical outcome in the tragedy of to-day.

Because most human beings possess what is popularly known as a "divine spark," the ideal of love has inevitably and perpetually made its appeal. When, at a comparatively late stage of development, humanity is capable of the atrocious cruelty displayed by the Bolshevik leaders towards the Russian intelligentsia, and by the Nazi rulers towards the Jews under their control, there are pathological explanations, familiar to every psychologist, in a previous history of frustration, persecution and suppression. Men and women inspired by charity and great generosity are alone capable of surviving persecution and humiliation without developing the vindictive desire for revenge. But though the essential decency of human nature is attracted by love as a virtue, it is only the few who have deliberately sacrificed the profits of power to the integrity of the spirit.

"Pity is a rebel passion," wrote Professor Gilbert Murray in his Introduction to *The Trojan Women,* that immortal threnody for the guiltless victims of battle which Euripedes wrote in the midst of the Peloponnesian War. "Its hand is against the strong, against the organised force of society, against conventional sanctions and accepted gods. It is the Kingdom of Heaven within us fighting against the brute powers of the world."

There is nothing harder for humanity to achieve than

the change of values which will permit it to be ruled by this rebel passion; to accept the standards of the Kingdom of Heaven in exchange for the rewards of privilege and power. Men and women will see their homes and their countries destroyed, and their children sacrificed to the insatiable Moloch of modern warfare, rather than face the hard and bitter thinking which will compel them to repudiate their traditions and reconstruct their ideals. This, and nothing less, is the "mental strife" which Blake enjoins on us in his *Jerusalem*—a strife from which, on occasion after occasion, we vow that "we will not cease" without realising that for most of us it has never begun.

"On the day of this war's end," the leading article in a left-wing London daily newspaper piously asserted of "our fighting men" a few weeks ago, "they will begin a new task—to widen and fortify the freedom they have defended; to secure justice for all races and all classes; to vanquish the oppression of economic dictatorship, even as they have vanquished armed dictatorship; to march swiftly on from Liberty to Equality and Fraternity."

This admirable programme is not of itself enough; we shall not achieve even one of these noble ends, if, at the conclusion of this war, we return, under whatever reassuring banner, to the old game of international power politics. We may conquer the foe which has scarred the face of London; we may make the usual good resolutions to build a new city and abolish the bombing aeroplane; but our victory alone will never enable us to re-create England and Europe. Much less will it teach us how to "build Jerusalem" unless the end of the struggle is followed by a total reconstruction of values such as the nations and their leaders had neither the courage nor the imagination to face in 1918.

It is, I am convinced, in the painful cultivation of personal humility and charity in every difficult relationship of human life, that our endeavours to found our City of God must now begin. We are entitled to seek for its practical cornerstones in such expedients as enlightened housing schemes and the repudiation of chemical warfare, but these and similar political measures could already have saved our civilisation from the present nightmare if enough of us had cultivated the *will* to adopt them. The foundations of our New Jerusalem depend not upon material programmes, but upon the acceptance of the ideal of love as the guiding principle of personal and national life.

That the change can be accomplished if we really desire it, and that the initiative can come from our own sorrowful but undaunted country, I have never doubted even in its darkest hours of complacency and self-seeking. Today, after witnessing London's endurance of its crucifixion without panic or vindictiveness, I am more than ever confident that the British people—provided that their innate decency is neither destroyed by the propaganda of hatred nor warped by excess of avoidable suffering—is better able than any people in the world to accept a way of life determined by love rather than by power.

"We beseech thee to take us as we are, and of thy mercy make us what thou wouldst have us be."

If we, as a nation, can accept the lesson which the minds that rule St. Paul's Cathedral have learned from its near escape from destruction, then England's hour may lead her from the power of darkness to the dawn of a new day.

The End

COMMON READER EDITIONS

As booksellers since 1986, we have been stocking the pages of our monthly catalogue, A COMMON READER, with "Books for Readers with Imagination." Now as publishers, the same motto guides our work. Simply put, the titles we issue as COMMON READER EDITIONS are volumes of uncommon merit which we have enjoyed, and which we think other imaginative readers will enjoy as well. While our selections are as personal as the act of reading itself, what's common to our enterprise is the sense of shared experience a good book brings to solitary readers. We invite you to sample the wide range of COMMON READER EDITIONS, and welcome your comments.

www.commonreader.com

A COMMON READER'S LONDON LIBRARY

England's Hour is the second volume in A COMMON READER'S LONDON LIBRARY. It is our hope that the books we choose for this series will, like this one, rank among the best ever written about London, and be of enduring interest to all those who are fascinated by the city and its storied history. The editors invite suggestions from readers for other out-of-print titles to be considered for inclusion in the LIBRARY.

ALSO IN A COMMON READER'S LONDON LIBRARY:
Nairn's London